D0421339

TEACHING AT UNIVERSITY

A Guide for Postgraduates and Researchers

Kate Morss
and Rowena Murray

SAGE Publications

London • Thousand Oaks • New Delhi

© Kate Morss and Rowena Murray 2005

First published 2005

Apart from any fair dealing for the purposes of research or
private study, or criticism or review, as permitted under
the Copyright, Designs and Patents Act, 1988, this publication
may be reproduced, stored or transmitted in any form, or by
any means, only with the prior permission in writing of the
publishers, or in the case of reprographic reproduction, in
accordance with the terms of licences issued by the Copyright
Licensing Agency. Inquiries concerning reproduction
outside those terms should be sent to the publishers.

SAGE Publications Ltd
1 Oliver's Yard
55 City Road
London EC1Y 1SP

SAGE Publications Inc.
2455 Teller Road
Thousand Oaks, California 91320

SAGE Publications India Pvt Ltd
B-42, Panchsheel Enclave
Post Box 4109
New Delhi 110 017

British Library Cataloguing in Publication data

A catalogue record for this book is available
from the British Library

ISBN 1 4129 0296 7
ISBN 1 4129 0297 5 (pbk)

Library of Congress Control Number: 2005924495

Typeset by C&M Digitals (P) Ltd., Chennai, India
Printed on paper from sustainable resources
Printed in Great Britain by TJ International, Padstow, Cornwall

Contents

Preface: A New Role

This book has been written primarily for postgraduates who are beginning to teach in higher education. We believe it is important that postgraduates have good support for developing their roles as teachers and facilitators of learning. That there is a need for this book is evidenced by requests for support and information from postgraduates. While lecturers usually have access to courses and workshops, postgraduates and other researchers are often not included in such programmes and they may not know where to get help.

The book is based on our experience, over a number of years, of developing and supporting postgraduates to become knowledgeable and confident in their teaching roles. We know that, faced with the thought of meeting their students imminently, postgraduates are often desperate for 'hints and tips'. We understand that need, and have included strategies, suggestions, guidelines, templates and questions or prompts for thinking. However, we believe that postgraduates should develop their teaching through the deliberate integration of theory and educational research with their practice and by becoming reflective practitioners.

Confidence building is equally important. If you have been left to your own devices, you are likely not to feel entirely comfortable in your new role. You will probably have to balance teaching with research and other activities. You will have to think carefully about how much time you spend on preparing for teaching, for example, so that it does not delay completion of your degree. This may mean improving your time management.

Alternatively, and equally importantly, there are examples of postgraduates who have been asked to take on more than they can manage – through either ability or availability – and we alert you at several points in our book to the need for clarity in role definition. In fact, we encourage you not to take on more than you feel you can manage, particularly if teaching is going to interfere with completion of the thesis; you might avoid problems later if you learn where, when and how to draw the line.

The aims of this book are to give you:

- introduction to the basics;
- explanation of different aspects of teaching;
- illustrations of good practice;

- frameworks for designing materials and classes;
- guidance on delivery of teaching;
- sources and resources for additional help;
- prompts to help you clarify your role and work out the limits of your abilities and responsibilities.

The book achieves these aims by providing:

- information in a clear accessible style;
- summaries of learning theories and models;
- references to key research data and seminal works;
- reference to relevant contemporary issues in higher education;
- focus on potential crises of confidence for postgraduate teachers;
- outlines of key forms of teaching;
- clear descriptions of practical, effective strategies;
- tips on what *not* to do and what might be problematic at this stage;
- coverage of all stages in teaching, from design to delivery;
- 'health warnings' – avoiding situations that are, arguably, problematic for postgraduates and/or where formal training is required.

The scope of this book is wide, since it covers many processes postgraduate teachers are likely to be involved in and topics they need to know about, such as current theory and best practice, guidelines and frameworks, concise summaries of debates. However, there are many specific ideas to help you deal with the realities of starting to teach.

To ensure the book will be useful in all disciplines, the content is generic, although we have cited specific examples from a wide range of subject areas.

What is not included are detailed discussions of theories and topics we consider to be outside the responsibilities of postgraduates, such as curriculum design and programme development, academic administration, and design and management of assessment.

This book is not intended to be a substitute for a course on teaching and learning in higher education. It is a handbook primarily designed to support those who, for whatever reason, do not have access to such a course before their first teaching assignment. However, for postgraduates lucky enough to receive some professional development and/or mentoring for teaching, the book will be a useful additional resource.

Acknowledgements

We would like to acknowledge all those postgraduates with whom we have worked over the years and thank them for their discussions, opinions and feedback on our courses and workshops. They have enabled us to stay in touch with what it is like to be a postgraduate teacher in the current higher education environment, and their comments have informed the writing of this book.

We thank those postgraduates and colleagues who dedicated their time and attention to read the draft of the book and give us helpful feedback: Donald Maciver, Christine Sinclair, Morag Thow, Bill Johnston, Beth McKay, Jane Hislop, Paul Maharg.

Introduction

Who is this book for?

This book is primarily aimed at postgraduate students who are just beginning to teach. So, you may be one of those students studying for a masters degree or a doctorate. These are the students we refer to throughout the book as 'postgraduates'. In some institutions, perhaps your own, postgraduates who teach may be called postgraduate teaching assistants (PGAs), demonstrators or some other title; to minimise confusion we have avoided these titles. We think this book will also be useful for postdoctoral students, contract researchers, teaching fellows or instructors and research staff – in short, for anyone whose main activity is research but who does some teaching at the same time.

If you have been asked to do some teaching, you may feel you have been 'thrown in at the deep end', as, in fact, many postgraduates tell us they are. You may, quite rightly, feel unprepared for the task, and, like other postgraduate teachers, you may be facing a number of dilemmas. For example, you may not have much time to feel your way into this new role. You may not be happy with what looks like a 'trial and error' model of learning to teach. You may even feel you have not had much choice in what you are to teach or what kinds of sessions you've been asked to facilitate.

Someone in your department may have tried to reassure you – 'You know all this stuff. You'll be fine' – on the basis of your first degree, but you may still be worried about whether or not you are really ready to teach.

We hope this book will support postgraduates in all disciplines, and for that reason we have kept its language generic. In acknowledgement of the sciences, we have included a chapter on teaching laboratories and fieldwork. For postgraduates who are engaged in highly experiential activities, such as conservatoire teaching in the arts, much of this book will be applicable.

Do you know what you are getting into?

Before you accept your first teaching task, consider the implications carefully. Yes, it is excellent for your professional development and for the curriculum vitae, especially if you intend to pursue an academic career, but teaching takes up time, in preparation, delivery and, frequently, marking. How much time can you afford at this stage of your research? How often will you need to be 'out', collecting data? How much data analysis will you need to do and how long is that likely to take? How much writing have you managed to do already and how much do you still have to do? When are the 'pressure points' for teaching and assessment, and how do they intercalate with your research schedule? How much 'new' work will you need to do in order to teach the topic(s)? Will you have to devise lectures and/or activities for group learning, laboratory work and individual study, or has all that already been done? What is the nature and volume of the assessments you may have to mark? See if you can get answers to at least some of these questions.

You may or may not have much room for negotiation about whether or not to teach, since some institutions require postgraduates to 'do a little teaching'. However, having thought through the answers to some of the questions we pose above, you should be better placed to set boundaries on what you do, and to position that work in the context of your research project. For example, we would suggest that you should draw the line at curriculum design and development, which really should not be your responsibility. These tasks should be handled by academic staff, since they require formal training and/or mentoring and discussion with department colleagues. In your discussions with staff about your teaching, you may be pressurised to do more than is fair or more than you want to do. Remember, however, that the priority, for both you and your research supervisors, is for you to complete your research on time.

To clarify, the accompanying table sets out responsibilities that are typical of most postgraduate teachers and could serve as a useful guide against which to benchmark your own commitments. You can see from this table that your primary roles may include the facilitation, support and/or assessment of students' learning. How much autonomy you will have in these roles will depend on your department and the institution. You may be asked to use pre-prepared PowerPoint slides for lectures and 'off the shelf' teaching materials for tutorials, or, in contrast, you may be given lots of freedom to 'do your own thing' as long as you cover the syllabus.

Regardless of the level of autonomy, it is your responsibility to help students learn as best you can. In order to do this well, you need to understand some of the theory and research on adult learning. You will need to know how programmes or courses run, how they relate to aims and objectives or learning outcomes, and where your particular teaching sits in the bigger picture of the whole curriculum. It is not enough to see one session or class in isolation and

Typical responsibilities of postgraduate teachers

WHAT IS YOUR RESPONSIBILITY	WHAT IS NOT YOUR RESPONSIBILITY
Know and use key research and theories on adult learning	Read every paper on the topic
Understand the programme/module aims and objectives/outcomes	Design the curricula
Stay on track with the syllabus	Write/rewrite the syllabus
Plan and prepare for your teaching	
Facilitate students' learning	Take responsibility for them
Help students prepare for assessments	
Provide information about assessments and criteria	Design the assessments
Assess fairly and give constructive feedback	
Return assessments promptly	
Comply with regulations and procedures for managing assessments and marks	Manage procedures for assessments and marking
Practise with due regard to the principles of and legislation on equal opportunities, race relations and disabilities	

plan to teach it as a discrete event. Above all, it is crucial that the learning and teaching activities you decide to use are linked to academic outcomes and assessments.

One area to which you should pay particular attention relates to the issues of equal opportunities, race relations and disabilities. In many countries now, there is legislation preventing discrimination on the basis of race, religion, ethnicity, gender, sexuality, disability and/or status, and you should know what the law requires in your country. You can, and should, find out more about these laws by asking your institution's policy unit or human resources department or by searching your government's website. However, regardless of the law, we strongly believe it is the responsibility of all educators to engage in practice which is inclusive and equitable. There is more discussion about these issues in Chapter 7 of this book which we encourage you to read. Other good places to start for information and pragmatic suggestions are *Accessible Curricula: Good Practice for All* (Doyle and Robson, 2002) (also available at the University of Wales Institute website http://www.uwic.ac.uk/ltsu/accessible.html) and the Teachability Project website of the University of Strathclyde (http://www.teachability.strath.ac.uk/).

Equal opportunities and inclusivity

It is your responsibility to be inclusive in your teaching, and there should be people in your institution whose responsibility it is to help you do this. They are the experts. You may find them in your university's student services department.

Things are moving so fast in this area, and are being applied differently in different universities, that we advise you to check this area for yourself. It is not that you should learn up all the law, but that you should learn about how it is being applied in your department.

Think about how you will ensure that you meet your institution's requirements in each of the forms of teaching covered in this book or, at least, in the form(s) of teaching you are required to do.

What do postgraduates say they need?

In this book, the topics covered and the weighting given to each topic were influenced by discussions and workshops with postgraduates. We have considered and responded to their concerns and explicitly included their questions and reactions throughout. The overwhelming message they give us, initially, is how much they want to learn about strategies, approaches, ideas and techniques they can use for planning and facilitating learning. The following quotes represent the most frequent responses when we asked postgraduates in 2001–5 what they would like our courses to cover:

Presentation style, facilitating discussions and asking questions to get answers.

How to select the most appropriate teaching method.

Preparing and structuring lessons, managing groups, feedback to students.

Managing tutorials, lecturing, assessment.

Demonstrating in practicals.

How to deal with situations when things go wrong.

After they engage in our courses and workshops, postgraduates say how useful that practical information has been, but they also say how much their thinking about learning has been changed by discussions based on research and theory. Some also appreciate that it is important to be aware of the wider issues in academic life, such as institutional regulations and procedures and national policies and codes of practice.

Lastly, but not least, some postgraduates express concern about how they will juggle teaching and research, especially if they think they will have to 'read up' on the subject(s) they have been asked to teach. This can, of course, be a very real problem, and one that we have tried to address throughout.

This is one of the risks we alert you to in what we call our 'health warnings'. They appear distinctly in boxes to warn you to think carefully about, for example, whether you are in danger of taking on too much or of straying, with the best of intentions, beyond your remit. We included these because postgraduates tell us that there are risks that they wish they had known about earlier, such as when, looking back, they know that they spent far too long preparing their first lesson. This may have been because they had no clear system of preparing and no criteria for judging what they were doing – a recipe for overinvestment of time and energy. What you do about these issues is, of course, for you to judge. Finding the balance between teaching and research, in your time management, is not easy, but we make suggestions throughout about when you need to pause and think through what you are doing, or even if you should be doing it.

What is this book about?

The first experience of teaching can be very stressful and even good, experienced teachers say they still feel nervous and anxious the first time they meet a new class. However, these experienced teachers also say their nervousness soon disappears; this is because they have skills and strategies, underpinned by an understanding of theory, for quickly establishing rapport and focusing on the learning and teaching.

With that in mind, this book offers a balance of theoretical and practical information to help you prepare for, practise and develop your teaching. It is intended to be used by those who have to survive primarily on their own devices, but it can also be a supplement to local training, mentoring and other forms of support. It is based on the premise that, ultimately, it is your responsibility to develop your understanding and practice of learning and teaching.

In order to do that, you have not only to develop practical skills but also to begin to grasp some of the principles of teaching and learning in higher education and to know something about the research. In this book we have worked hard not to submerge you in educational theory; instead, we provide key concepts and practical approaches for you to use. We do this by giving you:

- summaries of basic theories and models;
- explanations of different aspects of teaching;
- examples of good practice;
- frameworks you can use to design materials and classes;
- guidance and suggestions to help you facilitate learning;
- sources and resources for additional help;
- prompts for clarifying your role and working out your responsibilities;
- a framework for building your reflective teaching portfolio.

The aim, therefore, is not just for you to 'survive' the first teaching assignment, but for you to learn and develop in the course of that first experience. This comment from one of our postgraduates (2002) expresses her appreciation of that concept:

I've learned that teaching is a constantly changing process and involves a lot of reflection to become adept and a good teacher.

In fact, your first experience of teaching is the start of your development as a teacher, the point at which you begin to work out what you must or want to learn about teaching and learning. Documenting that first experience is therefore an important part of your development, and where you document it is in your teaching portfolio. Since many postgraduates tell us they do not know what this means, and since it is one way in which you can demonstrate that you have taken a professional approach to your teaching, we begin by defining it here and suggest ways in which you can build your portfolio at the end of each chapter.

Setting up your teaching portfolio

The portfolio is to teaching what lists of publications, grants and honors are to research and scholarship. (Seldin, 1997)

This is one definition of a teaching portfolio which describes it as both a collection of work and evidence of work. There is now a considerable amount of literature on teaching portfolios, but there is debate about what a portfolio is and how you compile one.

However, because you are about to embark on another learning journey, that is learning about learning, teaching and assessment, our view of a teaching portfolio is that it must include a critical and reflective appraisal of your own practice supported by the evidence of that practice. In other words, putting student evaluation forms or copies of articles about teaching into a shoebox or folder is not enough. What is important is that you:

- think in advance about what you want to know and plan how you will collect evidence;
- collect the evidence;
- critically reflect on the evidence to see what your students are learning and how you are teaching;
- decide what you will do next and plan for future action.

You will have many opportunities to accumulate piles of paper and other types of evidence, such as videos, but our suggestion is that you should be deliberate and selective about what you choose. Furthermore, your choices will change as you move through your career.

The reflective portfolio is an excellent way to track your own learning and plan your professional development (Moon, 1999; 2004). However, it may also prove to be a useful document in applying for jobs, promotions, memberships of professional bodies and honorary recognition. Already, a number of professional bodies require teaching portfolios to maintain membership, and many institutions require membership of the relevant professional association.

You can start this now. You can begin thinking about the learning journey you have started in reading this chapter by doing some writing to the following prompts:

- What I read: summary of this chapter, highlighting what were, for you, the main point(s).
- What I got out of that section/paragraph/discussion, including questions it raised.
- I discussed this with a colleague/mentor (summarise). I have a better understanding and/or new questions about certain issues.
- What I plan to do next: further reading/discussion/action.

1

Theory and Practice

I've always, sort of done things according to my gut feelings and never been really sure it was right. It's great to have some theory under my belt so I can think and plan my teaching better.

I don't even know where to start!

These remarks come from postgraduates who attend our courses on learning, teaching and assessment. The first is representative of individuals who have 'done a bit of teaching' already and have some experience behind them. The second is typical of a postgraduate who has never taught before, and may be facing a new class soon. Both comments reveal a certain lack of confidence which may arise from the need to know more about the research and theory base that underpins teaching in higher education.

If you study this chapter, which gives you selected, key information about current theories, models and research which most relate to the teaching of adults in higher education, you are much more likely to have the confidence of knowing you are acting on a sound knowledge base. You may also find, like many of our postgraduates, that you 'get hooked' on learning and teaching and want to learn more through long term, systematic engagement in professional development.

We begin with a brief explanation of why knowing something about theories of learning might help you. This is followed by a streamlined overview of theories and models of learning which you should find most useful and a summary of some key research on how adults learn, particularly in the context of higher education. In doing so, we mention the possible implications of this information for your teaching. There is a short section on methods for measuring what your students are actually learning – as opposed to what you might think, or hope, they are learning. This kind of formative feedback early in your teaching career can be both revealing and constructive for developing your teaching. Finally, there is a section on how you can use a theory base in your teaching portfolio.

We also introduce and define selected key terms which you will hear and read about and probably need to keep in your head. These terms are not jargon, although you may hear them called that; they are, instead, part of the specialised vocabulary of the discipline of learning and teaching. This means that you will have to start to work out how they apply to learning and teaching in your discipline.

What is the point of learning theory?

Increasing your confidence

Some postgraduates on our courses tell us they do not really want to bother with the theory, they just want to get on with talking about how to teach and deal with the problems they are worried about. However, discussions about theory are not just about the knowledge. Our observations are that they are more to do with the confidence they give you to know that what you are doing is grounded in research and theory, and that somebody else has checked that a particular theory works in practice. This is why more experienced teachers than you are often relieved to find that what they have been doing for years is in line with current research.

More importantly, some knowledge of theory will help you overcome the top three problems that postgraduates say they face in their first experiences as teachers:

1   not knowing enough about the subject and fear of not being able to answer questions – fear of lack of respect or overt disrespect;
2   not having a repertoire of strategies to get you out of problematic situations, for example when students will not participate in tutorials;
3   not having autonomy in your teaching role, so that you feel you cannot change anything that is not working.

It might be appropriate to feel you do not yet have credibility as a teacher, but understanding the research, the theory and a range of practices can help you establish credibility and overcome what we know are recurring problems.

Understanding your teaching role

Undergraduates often find that they can relate to postgraduates in a way that they cannot with academics. For example, they may feel you are closer to their world of undergraduate study and therefore able to talk to them about experiences you remember well. Significantly, because you are doing research yourself, you will be able to bridge research and teaching in a way that could be stimulating and exciting for undergraduates.

Thus, you may be in a unique position to influence, guide and support your students' learning in a way that others cannot. If you understand something about educational theory, you should be able to build on these advantages. For example, knowing the principles of constructivist learning (which we explain below), you could employ your expertise to guide students through a discussion on 'What is research?' starting from their everyday experiences, such as conducting research prior to purchasing a mobile phone.

With some theoretical background, you will be able to check for yourself that you have been addressing the intended learning outcomes, and that your strategies for facilitating learning have allowed students to practise the skills on which they will be assessed. Furthermore, because you are involved in teaching, assessment and/or student support, you will understand what people are talking about when they use the discourse of learning and teaching. This will mean that you will be able to converse meaningfully about these topics with the programme leader, module coordinator or your academic and postgraduate colleagues, and this will be a real boost for both your credibility and your confidence.

Informing decisions in practice

Even if you are 'told what to do' and have materials and a teaching schedule organised for you, you will still have decisions or choices to make. How you make these choices depends on learning outcomes, the student group, resources, the culture of your department and other factors. For example, suppose you are demonstrating a task to a group and some students do not 'get it'. Do you repeat your demonstration? What if they still do not 'get it'? Do you show them a third time? What if time is running out? What do you do? No schedule is going to answer all students' questions or suggest alternative strategies for you and, in any case, you may be alone with the class. It is up to you to find something that works – how would you go about doing that? This is the kind of scenario that normally scares new teachers who do not know what their options are, or who have a limited range of options to start with. Clearly, in this scenario, you would have to find other ways of getting your students to understand the task; demonstration alone is not going to work for everybody.

In some instances, you will have to make decisions about how you are going to teach – sometimes 'on the spot'. This is a complex task and your responsibility is to weave all the factors together to make the best decision; knowing more about how adults learn in your discipline can help. The benefit of this learning, for you, is that you gradually build your repertoire of strategies.

Informing your planning

You may find that you are given a substantial role in learning, teaching and assessment, and that you are expected to design, plan and implement learning opportunities for students. This could include lectures, tutorials, seminars, practicals, field trips, projects, web-based learning or any variations on these. Some postgraduates, for instance, are given responsibility for managing all the tutorials or labs in a semester for a module or subject. You will probably be given guidance, a schedule or syllabus, and further information, but you may find that you have more autonomy in how you go about teaching. In this case, you will need to know even more about theory and research, in order to avoid serious mistakes or time wasting. You should, however, try to work closely with a more experienced member of staff, just to check you are on track.

Because your need for guidance may be quite focused – perhaps even urgent – we do not intend to overview all research and theory related to learning, teaching and assessment. There are other books and resources to serve that purpose. Our aim is to get you thinking about how your students are learning. Thinking of your own experience will help, but we want to move beyond that to a cogent but systematic body of knowledge, so that you do not have to rely on an *ad hoc* collection of hints, tips and anecdotes. Your own experience as a learner is, of course, an important source of information about good and bad teaching, but there is much more information out there. Furthermore, at a time when key research is emerging that can inform good practice, we have no excuses for ignoring it.

Don't underestimate how difficult it is to put theory into practice. As you go about developing your teaching skills, look around you. How often do you **HEALTH WARNING** see the gap between theory, research and actual practice? How often is educational research actually discussed or even mentioned? For all of us, closing that gap is about paying close attention to continuous improvement. It is about building up a body of coherent experience. It involves failure, making sense of failure, trying again. This process may lead to solutions to teaching challenges, but it can just as often generate new questions.

FIGURE 1.1
Experiential learning cycle (Adapted from Kolb, 1984)

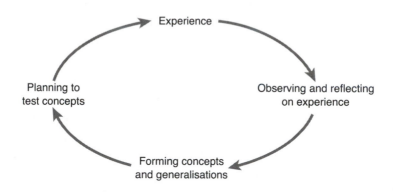

How do adults learn?

Experiential learning

As you begin to learn about teaching, an important starting point is to think about your experience as a learner. How do you learn? To begin your thinking on this question, consider something that you know you do well, like riding a bicycle, driving a car, playing a sport or a musical instrument. How did you learn to do that? What factors were important in that learning?

When we ask postgraduates this question, their responses always fall into these categories: doing it, practising (nearly 100% of respondents say that practice is essential); thinking back, reflecting on the experience; sorting out what went wrong, getting feedback; planning what to do next; doing it again. If you think about how you learned to do almost anything, you will probably find that this cycle of 'doing it' (playing an instrument or strategically placing a tennis ball in the opposite court), reflecting, reasoning (theorising about what went wrong) and planning (deciding what to do differently next time) applies to you. Could this be why we so often hear the phrase 'We learn from experience'? Linking the work of others with his own thinking, Kolb (1984) proposed the experiential learning cycle, a model of learning that incorporates these four stages (Figure 1.1). In our examples of learning given above, you can see how this experiential model of learning makes explicit what many people say about how they learn.

You may be thinking that these examples are simplistic and very skills oriented. That is arguable, but it might be more meaningful if you consider a more abstract example, such as how you are learning to do research. Yes, you will be reading, observing and talking to other researchers, planning your own methodologies, but you will also be 'doing' the research, reflecting on results, refining methodologies, planning the next phase, etc. Are you 'going round the cycle'?

We think Kolb's experiential learning model is one useful way of understanding what genuine learning involves – that we have to engage actively, to do a task, to try out, to practise; to think retrospectively about what we have done; to form theories or postulate why we got the result we did; and to plan again. Then we have to have time to 'go round the cycle', perhaps several – perhaps many – times. The learning is complex, of course, because it has at least three different components: it incorporates (1) learning 'that' (knowledge), (2) learning 'how' (skills) and (3) other aspects of learning related to judgement, values and attitudes. However, one feature of Kolb's model is the attention it draws to the importance of skills in learning, an aspect often forgotten in higher education.

The interesting thing about Kolb's experiential learning cycle is that it is also a constructive tool for designing your teaching. In thinking about planning a tutorial, for instance, you might divide the time into four subperiods, allowing students to engage in each of the stages of the cycle. For a longer period, perhaps there is time for them to repeat the cycle. Note that it is not necessary to start with the 'doing' stage; depending on what the learning outcomes and the nature of the activity are, you can start with any of the stages and work round the cycle.

However, our postgraduates categorically state that Kolb's cycle model lacks one key element essential for learning – motivation. On the basis of their own learning experiences, postgraduates insist that we insert motivational words such as 'want', 'need' and 'commitment' in the middle of the cycle in order to indicate the importance of motivation. As they see it, it should be in the centre of the model. They are, of course, quite right, and the relevance of motivation is captured in another model of learning, developed by Race (1993). Some of our postgraduates prefer this model to Kolb's. Race's model is easier to remember, for a start, and it re-presents Kolb's model with a different perspective. Figure 1.2 reproduces Race's initial thinking of learning as a cyclic process, and his revised model of learning represented by his 'ripples' model. You may prefer one of these models to Kolb's, but all of them provide helpful images for thinking about and planning for learning.

Constructivism

What postgraduates tell us is that they go around the learning cycle many times (an upward spiral) as they build on previous learning. This is one example of what we call constructivism. Constructivism is the term you can use to refer to the process of building up your own knowledge by connecting new information with

FIGURE 1.2
Race's models of learning (Race, 1993)

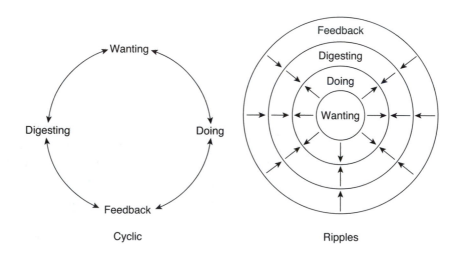

Cyclic   Ripples

what you know already and forming concepts, or constructs, which are models of reality (Biggs and Moore, 1993; Biggs, 2003; Prosser and Trigwell, 1999). As new knowledge and experiences are assimilated, knowledge structures grow and are modified. Because we all have different knowledge bases, with discrete connections between those knowledge elements, each of us has to scaffold our own learning for ourselves. For this to happen, we have to take an active role in our learning.

> **Constructivism:** the process of building up your own knowledge by connecting new information with what you know already and forming concepts that are models of reality.

New information has to link with what you know. Can you remember attending a lecture or a class in which you did not have a clue what the teacher was talking about? There is a good chance that this happened because you did not know the terminology or the literature and therefore had no 'pegs' or 'hooks' to which you could connect new information. It is possible that your teacher had made assumptions about what you, and the rest of the class, already knew and pitched the information at the wrong level. What can we learn from situations like this?

'The most important single factor influencing learning is what the learner already knows. Ascertain this and teach him accordingly' (Ausubel, 1968: 127). Ausubel, like others, recognised the importance of making connections between known concepts and new ones – that we need to support students to construct their knowledge and understanding by (1) starting from what they already know, and (2) planning learning opportunities which allow them to build up their learning, stepwise, in their own individual ways. This may seem straightforward to you now, but the phrase 'individual ways' hints that it is not as easy as it might first appear.

For your role, helping undergraduates to make connections – between what they learn in your class and what they know from elsewhere – and helping them to make sense of those connections, could be key. Exactly how we can prompt our students to be actively involved in their learning is the subject of a body of research. There is material out there to help us develop the techniques to do this.

Concepts of learning and approaches to study

Research on adult learning and learning in higher education is informing our understanding of the individual nature of learning and the factors which influence it. We give a brief summary of the main research findings below, but you should know that this is an area where the research literature is expanding rapidly.

Consider the comments on concepts of learning shown in the box. These quotes from Gibbs (1990) summarise the seminal research of Marton, Saljo and Entwistle (Marton, 1988; Marton and Saljo, 1976a; 1976b; Entwistle and Ramsden, 1983) and show that individual students can have quite different concepts of what learning involves. Student 1 seems to think that learning is memorising by repeatedly going over and over information. Student 2, on the other hand, is likely to look for patterns and underpinning principles, relating ideas to previous knowledge, and attempting to internalise the information so that he or she can express it in his or her own words. For student 3, learning is a profound experience, altering outlook and changing perspective.

Concepts of learning

Learning is about getting it into your head. You've just to keep writing it out and eventually it will go in. (student 1)

Learning is about trying to understand things so you can see what is going on. You've got to be able to explain things, not just remember them. (student 2)

When you have really learnt something you kind of see things you couldn't see before. Everything changes. (student 3)

(Gibbs, 1990)

Considerable research (Marton et al., 1997; Entwistle and Ramsden, 1983) has led to the conclusion that students have different approaches to study, that is, their intentions determine how they engage with a set learning task. Student 1 takes a 'surface' approach: memorising facts, reproducing information, failing to make connections between related ideas and concentrating on content. Students 2 and 3 take a 'deep' approach to learning: attempting to link ideas, examining the logic of an argument, checking evidence. These students are studying with intent to understand.

Which approach would you like to see your students taking? Most of us would say a deep approach is what learning at university should be about. The way we plan and carry out our teaching can help students to move towards deeper approaches to learning. However, we all know – or remember doing it ourselves – students who take a a 'strategic' approach (Biggs, 2003); we used surface learning when it served the purpose, and engaged in deep learning when challenged and/or stimulated to do so. Table 1.1 summarises the main characteristics of approaches to study.

While individuals may have their own approaches to learning, the context of that learning will influence how and what they learn (Ramsden, 1988). Surface

TABLE 1.1

Students' approaches to study

APPROACHES TO STUDY	CHARACTERISTICS
Surface	Memorising, reproducing facts, focus on content, assessment oriented
Deep	Examining argument, studying underlying principles or rationale, linking ideas and concepts
Strategic	Applying either of the above approaches to suit the outcomes, expectations and assessment

learning will be encouraged and reinforced by assessments which focus on recall, large amounts of material, low levels of application or relevance of the material, lack of background and limited independence or choice in study. Deep approaches to learning will be stimulated by challenging assessments, teaching which stresses meaning and relevance to students, opportunities for choice, interest in and background to the subject matter, and explicit, clearly stated academic expectations (Ramsden, 2003).

How do these ideas apply to the teaching and learning situations you know? Can you recognise how individuals work in different ways? If you are already teaching, have you observed that your students try to write down everything you say in class and then copy it all out again? Do they reproduce the notes you have given them in their assignments, with no personal commentary? Do they frequently ask to see you to check they are 'on the right lines' and ask questions for clarification? Do they read and think for so long before starting to write that they cannot finish their assignments? These kinds of sensitive observations should stimulate you to think about how you can help students understand, and work with, their own approaches to learning.

It is important to stress here that surface learning is not always a bad thing, and may sometimes be necessary. Your students may need to memorise terminology, as in anatomy or microbiology, or important names and dates, as in history, or vocabulary, as in languages. In these circumstances, students may be unable to communicate in the discipline if they have not converted the required information to memory. What we are saying is, think about what kind of learning is appropriate when, and think about how the learning approaches should be valued.

Learning styles

Although people do not, of course, fall into neat categories, it is reasonably well established that individuals do have preferred learning styles. You may be familiar with Honey and Mumford's (1982) learning styles questionnaires, which present four categories of learner: pragmatist, activist, reflector and theorist. The pragmatist is practical and logical, whereas the activist is eager to get on with the task – a doer. The reflector will hold back to think and plan, whereas the theorist will read, research, find models and theories to follow. Clearly, people do not fit exclusively one category, but it is surprising how often they do say their Honey and Mumford profiles are typical of their behaviour and demonstrate their learning styles. What is your learning style? Do you know?

Other researchers have similar categories, such as the serialist (operational learning), holist (comprehension learning) and versatile learning described by Pask (1976). Still others remind us that some people learn best through pictures and diagrams (visual), some prefer words on the page (verbal), others need to hear (oral) and still others are kinesthetic learners, needing to 'do'.

However, why is all this important for you as a teacher? In a room (real or virtual) full of students there will be those who have different learning styles. Furthermore, you undoubtedly have a preferred learning style too, which will affect the activities you organise for students. How will you handle this? What do you need to do? The implication of this research for new teachers is that if you only have one way of doing things, then almost inevitably you will lose the attention and/or engagement of some of the students in the room. This is not to say you should be 'all-singing, all-dancing' for every minute of every class; clearly that is neither feasible nor sensible. However, there are lots of little things you can do that will support students with different learning styles – maybe not all at the same time.

One useful strategy is to make these points the subject of a brief discussion with students: would it not help them hugely to know what type of learners they are, what that means for their learning, and how you are trying to accommodate different learning styles, including your own, in your teaching? It might, therefore, be a good time to spend some time discussing personal learning styles, explain that you use different activities to accommodate those styles and point this out as you go along, so that they see what you mean. This does not mean giving the students a lecture on learning styles; you can make the point in less than a minute, then refer to them as you move on.

Perhaps both you and your students also need to acknowledge that there may be times when your students 'tune out', for whatever reason, and that this may not be your fault. On the other hand, it might be a moment where you encourage students to engage in an activity that does not seem to suit the majority's learning styles, because part of learning is moving outside their comfort zone.

> **Learning styles:**   these are indicators of individuals' preferred ways of learning. Learning styles can be categorised in a number of ways, depending on the researcher and the tools used to measure learning styles.

Social learning

So far, our discussions have centred on examining how individuals learn, looking at learning as an individual process. Clearly, learning also has a social dimension, since we learn from and with others in all our social interactions. You will be aware, from your own experiences, of how much you have learned outside of what you have been taught formally. This learning from social relationships is sometimes referred to as the 'hidden curriculum'.

People also learn as members of a group who share common goals and participate in collective learning. This kind of learning is mutual and proactive, not merely responsive, and is more than the sum of individuals' learning within the group (Jarvis et al., 2003).

The relevance of this to you in your teaching role is that it prompts you to recognise and allow social learning to happen. Often students learn from each other, by observing and 'copying' behaviour, through peer tutoring or through 'vicarious' learning during group work (Bandura, 1986). You should positively encourage, if not exploit, these effective methods of learning.

Having read a little about theories, models and research on learning in higher education, you may be tempted to jump to subsequent chapters on lecturing, group learning, etc. – especially if your learning style is activist or pragmatist. However, the next section contains information and advice that will prove crucial in orienting yourself within the higher education teaching environment and, importantly, in helping you to become an effective facilitator of learning.

What is the curricular framework for learning and teaching in higher education?

For a number of years, learning and teaching in higher education in many countries have been driven by curricula based on a set of aims and specific objectives or goals to be achieved by learners but defined by teachers. More recently, there has been a shift in focus from objectives to outcomes, that is specific statements of what learners will know and be able to do as a result of their learning. Generally, aims and learning outcomes are described by the educators, very much less frequently by the learners. A framework based on aims and learning outcomes provides a useful structure for guiding learning and assessment but there are those who argue that it constrains, even inhibits, the individual's learning and freedom to explore (Jarvis, 2004).

Constructive alignment

Biggs (2003) proposed a curricular framework, now widely adopted in the higher education sector, which links the theory of constructive learning to an outcomes-based approach. This model, called constructive alignment, arises from two key principles:

1 Learning and teaching should be 'learner centred'. Because individual learners must construct their own learning, it is 'what the learner does' that is most important.
2 Aims and learning outcomes, learning and teaching activities and assessment must be aligned so that learners know what is to be achieved, how they will engage in activities which will help them achieve those outcomes, and how they will demonstrate they have done so. This alignment is necessary to provide a transparent framework within which individual learning is constructed.

Thus, constructive alignment enables students to construct their own learning by ensuring that, within the curriculum, aims, learning outcomes, learning and teaching activities and assessment are matched.

> **Constructive alignment:**   the deliberate linking, within curricula, of aims, learning outcomes, learning and teaching activities and assessment. Learning outcomes state what is to be achieved in fulfilment of the aims; learning activities should be organised so that students will be likely to achieve those outcomes; assessment must be designed such that students are able to demonstrate they have met the learning outcomes.

Setting aims and learning outcomes gives students real, tangible goals so they know what they have to know and be able to do – you could say it eliminates the guesswork. Aligning the assessment with the learning outcomes means they know how their achievements will be measured. Then, planning and designing the learning – without getting hung up on the 'teaching' – gives students opportunities to develop their knowledge and skills and to practise for their assessment. How else will they learn what they need to know and do? The concept of aligning aims, outcomes, assessment and learning and teaching strategies seems so simple that some might say this is just a fancy name for 'joining up the dots'. The trouble is, very often it does not happen in practice.

Let us say that a learning outcome for students might be that they should be able to critique a paper. However, how often do they get a chance to do

FIGURE 1.3
Alignment for constructive learning (Based on Biggs, 2003 and Moon, 1999)

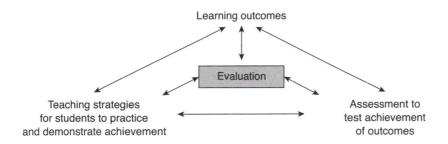

that – once, ever? Is that enough? Do we ever show them how to do it? Do we give them criteria or a set of questions to provide a framework? Maybe not. Yet this outcome may be assessed by asking students to critique an unseen paper as part of an examination. In this case, the assessment is aligned with the learning outcomes, but the learning (and teaching) is not aligned.

Alternatively, if the learning outcome is that students should be able to critique a paper, but the assessment is that they should write an essay summarising research methodologies for qualitative research, it is obvious that the assessment is misaligned with the learning outcome. This is, quite frankly, unfair to students. It turns learning and assessment into a guessing game – one that, arguably, has been going on for too long.

Alignment, therefore, is essential to ensure that students are not misled, and to make the learning and assessment process as transparent to them as possible. Furthermore, we would add that constant evaluation is crucial to the maintenance of that alignment. Figure 1.3 demonstrates the relationship between these elements: the curriculum, learning, teaching and evaluation.

Aims and learning outcomes

Aims are broad statements of intent or purpose, such as 'The aim of this module is to enable students to develop their oral and written communication skills in various business contexts.' Words commonly used in aims are enable, support, facilitate, introduce, review and outline, because they describe the overall intentions of the staff who write them. Learning outcomes are specific statements of what students should know or be able to do as a result of the learning. They are statements describing observable behaviour and therefore must use 'action verbs'. There are literally hundreds of action verbs, including: name, list, describe, discuss, draw, construct, measure, calculate, summarise, justify and evaluate. All learning outcomes should be SMART: specific, measurable, achievable, realistic and relevant, and time limited. This means that they should be specific enough for students to know exactly what they need to do, so that staff can measure whether students have done it, so that the outcomes are achievable within the time they have (for example, a semester) and so that they are relevant to the aims of the course.

> **Aims:**   broad statements which clarify the intent or purpose of a course, module or learning activity.
>
> **Learning outcomes:**   specific statements of what students should know and be able to do as a result of learning.

Some aims and learning outcomes typical of a module, for example a one-semester course of study, are shown below. What is your assessment of these learning outcomes? Do they align with the aims? Are they SMART? If you were a student on this module, would you know what you were expected to know and do? Two words you may find used to describe learning outcomes are 'appreciate' and 'understand'. What does 'appreciate' mean – to know a little bit about, to applaud, to be thankful for? How do we measure 'understanding' and how do students 'demonstrate' that to us – by discussing, debating, applying tools and/or concepts? In our view, these are terms which do not help students because there are so many interpretations of their meaning. It is more transparent, and helpful, to be specific about expectations. However, these words are often used by academic staff in writing learning outcomes. If you are teaching and/or assessing to these types of outcomes, you might need to discuss them with staff to ensure you have a shared interpretation.

Example module: aim and learning outcomes

Aim

The aim of this module is to enable students to develop knowledge and skills of research necessary to complete a small-scale research project.

Learning outcomes

Upon successful completion of the module, students should be able to:

- set an apposite and feasible research question;
- select, analyse and synthesise relevant published literature;
- design and write an appropriate research proposal;
- plan and conduct the investigation using an appropriate research method;
- analyse, interpret and present data;
- discuss the meaning of their findings;
- write up the research in a report according to given guidelines.

Suppose you discover that aims and outcomes are not well written and possibly not aligned with assessment? What do you do:

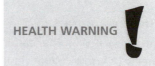

HEALTH WARNING

- nothing;
- discuss it with module coordinator or course leader;
- change it yourself;
- press on?

This may be the biggest challenge in teaching a course someone else has designed. Can you challenge the status quo? It is risky, but the point is to enhance learning for your students. Therefore, what exactly should you say? How can you raise this positively? Your best approach might be to express your own uncertainties about whether your students will be able to demonstrate they have met the learning outcomes. This could be a good opener for a productive discussion with the module coordinator or course leader. If you have thought of an alternative assessment which would be better, you might suggest it. However, unless you have been designated the module coordinator, it is not your responsibility to make the major changes, which in most institutions take considerable time.

> If the course is not aligned and you decide you have to get on with it, what do you do? You have to do your best to ensure your students are able to practise the things they will be assessed on, so that will shape what you do in the classroom. This may mean taking a particular interpretation of the outcomes and finding some way of aligning them with the assessment. It may require emphasising one or more of the outcomes over the others. Importantly, you will have to be able to articulate that to yourself or others, for example, in your teaching portfolio, mentoring or other discussions.

What next?

Planning and designing for learning

The obvious place to start with planning and designing learning opportunities for students is with the learning outcomes and the assessment. What do your students need to know? What do they need to do? What skills must they demonstrate? What cognitive abilities must they display? How will the assessment measure these things? Then, having answered these questions, what will you do to enable them to acquire the knowledge and process it, and to develop and refine their skills? What, then, do you need to do to set up situations so they can do that?

Therefore, if students will be required to critique a paper as their final assessment in order to achieve the learning outcomes, here are some initial ideas for structuring their learning:

- discuss what is meant by 'critique' and how you begin to do that;
- deconstruct, with them, a published critique of another paper;
- design (with their input) a set of criteria or guidelines to help them with the task;
- find suitable papers in the literature for them to practise on;
- get them to peer review a critique written by a classmate and conduct a plenary discussion about the key principles and issues.

If you just do a lecture on 'How to critique a paper', they will probably not ever practise doing it; they may not even know which paper to select or where to find it, or possibly will just never 'get around to it'. Clearly, the lecture is a 'teacher-centred' process which focuses on what the teacher does. If, however, you start with what students should be doing and what they are likely to learn from that activity, the emphasis shifts to how you set up and facilitate situations which enable the students to learn what you want them to or what the course coordinator wants them to.

Motivating learners

One of the factors affecting learning which we mentioned above referred to motives. You will know from your own experience that people may be motivated to learn for many different reasons: they may want a qualification as a reward and/or symbol of achievement or as the entry point to a job or promotion. Some students are motivated to learn out of genuine interest and love of learning. Most are motivated by the assessment, as we will see in Chapter 6. You will find that motivation is a powerful driver for learning (Brown et al., 1998). It will make your experience and your students' experiences more enjoyable, even fun, if you can keep your students motivated to learn. This is not always an easy task, of course, but keeping your attention on what they are doing will prompt you to plan activities which are relevant, engaging, interesting and challenging. Remember, it is what students do that is important.

In practice, probably the best way to determine if your students are motivated is to watch them. Are they animated and talking about the subject? Do they ask questions? Do they talk about the subject during the break? Do they try to talk to you about the subject after class? When they write, is there evidence that they have done some reading? By consistently observing their behaviour, you can begin to judge what it is that stimulates their learning and you can make connections with the way you designed activities; in short, you can see what works and what does not. As you continue to learn about teaching, observe your students, think about how they are learning, think about how you will respond on the basis of what you are learning about teaching – and that will embed theory into your practice.

Measuring your students' learning

In this chapter, we have emphasised the centrality of student learning which is carefully planned and facilitated. But of course you will want to know how successful your efforts are. What are your students getting out of the class? Are they learning what you hope they are? Are the activities you planned engaging students in the way you expected? There may be a million questions you want to ask so that you get plenty of feedback. Throughout this book, and especially in Chapter 10, we suggest ways in which you can evaluate students' learning as well as collect feedback on your teaching so that you can continually improve your practice. This will also be important information for your teaching portfolio.

However, here are two simple, quick and effective evaluative tools which you can incorporate into your first teaching plans.

Give each student three Post-it notes. On one they should write 'learned', on another 'appreciate' and on the third 'regret'. Ask your students to write a response to the prompt on each Post-it, and to stick the Post-its on the door or wall as they leave the room. You collect and sort them and quickly learn something about what they are thinking about both the learning and the teaching (or something else entirely, for example, food). Obviously, you may use any number of variations of this Post-it method of evaluation to get feedback on both learning and teaching (such as 'stop', 'start', 'continue').

Another very successful tool to evaluate learning is to ask the students to write a note or short letter to a friend about what they are learning in your class. This inserts an element of informality into the evaluation and can give you some genuine insights.

Portfolio

We introduced the concept of a teaching portfolio in the introduction to this book. Here, as in each of the following chapters, we suggest ideas for building your portfolio as you go. This will not only document your learning journey, but also provide you with a 'bitesize' approach.

What you might do now, to get your teaching portfolio moving, is to write about reading this chapter:

- What ideas have stimulated your thinking?
- How do they relate to your own experiences of learning?
- Do you know what your own learning style is?
- What other reading have you done? What was meaningful for you and why?
- Who have you talked to about learning and teaching in your discipline?

This is just the start of a series of ongoing conversations. They need not be jargon laden. They need not be long. You might not even discuss the terms used in this chapter, explicitly. The point is you need to find out which ideas, models, and theories are being used in your subject now. What are they based on? How do they happen? What research influenced them? Who can you have the conversation with about them? Talking to lecturing staff, consulting your postgraduate colleagues and chatting to students are all interesting ways of learning more about learning and teaching.

However, it is up to you to make some connection between the theory and the teaching being done in your subject. If you can document that, you have some excellent material for your portfolio.

Ultimately, however, it needs to be related to your own practice. Think back over your planning for teaching. Have you made opportunities and time for your students to go round Kolb's experiential learning cycle? Will they have a chance to reflect, form concepts and plan for the next round? When have you tried to connect new knowledge with what they may know already?

Lastly, what reading and web searching have you been doing? Some references are suggested in the following:

Additional resources

Atherton, J.S. (2003) *Learning and Teaching: Learning Index.*
   http://www.dmu.ac.uk/~jamesa/learning/, accessed 21 February 2005.
This site provides an excellent and entertaining journey through learning theories. Our postgraduates like it.

Biggs, J. (2003) *Teaching for Quality Learning at University,* 2nd edn. Buckingham: SRHE and
   Open University Press.
Biggs sets out the principle of constructive alignment, succinctly covers relevant theories and deals with all the aspects of learning, teaching and assessment you are likely to need in an intelligent but accessible manner.

Higher Education Academy (HE Academy). http://www.heacademy.ac.uk.

Your First Lectures

I hate the thought of getting up in front of all those students. What if it all goes pear-shaped?

We open this chapter with the question of why you are lecturing and what you can actually achieve by lecturing. As part of this discussion we will refer to the best sources of research on learning from lectures – and this is one area where there is a fairly substantial body of research to stimulate your thinking. Then we will discuss how you can plan lectures to achieve the best outcomes for your students and, possibly, relieve some of the stress you may be feeling.

Postgraduates often tell us that it is 'doing' the lectures that causes them most anxiety, either because of a fear that something will go wrong or because something has gone wrong before. The advice we offer comes from our own and others' experiences of what works, but also from the increasing body of knowledge about what helps students to learn from lectures. It is intended to focus on the fundamental aspects of lecturing you may wish to consider so that all goes well when you stand in front of the class. In response to the common worries that postgraduates tell us about, we suggest some specific strategies and other sources of help to improve lecturing skills.

The two main points of this chapter are how to enhance your students' learning and how to improve your skills in lecturing. The obvious question arising, then, is how do you evaluate those two things? How do you know you are getting better? How do you know what students are learning? We propose simple strategies for measuring your students' learning from lectures. Lastly, we suggest things you can do to get feedback on your lecturing from students and colleagues, and how you can build this evidence into your teaching portfolio.

Why are you lecturing?

Joe has just asked me to give a series of lectures to second-year biology students. He just gave me the syllabus and said, 'All you need to do is cover these topics.'

So you have been asked to give one or more lectures. Where do you start, especially if this is something you've never done before? What questions should you ask?

First questions to ask about lecturing

- Who are you lecturing to and what subject are they studying?
- What level or year of study are the students in?
- How many students are there?
- Which topic(s) are to be addressed?
- How many lectures are there to be?
- When are they to be: what are the dates and times?
- How long are lecture sessions?
- Where are they to be held?
- What is the size of the room, layout of furniture and lighting?
- What presentation equipment is there?
- Will there be a microphone?
- Are there any disabled students who need support?

No doubt these are the first, practical, questions to come to you, and you'll want some answers before you go any further.

Talk to your module coordinator, course leader or tutor before, during and after you do your lecturing. Apart from discussing the questions above, you need to know more about who your students are: what is the level or year of study; what knowledge about the subject should they have already; what should you expect them to be able to do? You also need to discuss which part(s) of the syllabus you are expected to cover, and to discuss details about the depth and breadth of coverage. You will want to feel confident that you are adequately preparing students for their assessment and supporting disabled students appropriately (Doyle and Robson, 2002; SHEFC, 2000).

Other topics to discuss might be how you can check that you – and your students – are on track. These conversations will help to keep you 'connected' with the module coordinator or course leader, and will provide good opportunities for a collegial discussion about learning and teaching. This process of talking to your course leader about your teaching – before, during and after – establishes a useful habit that does not apply just to your postgraduate work; it should be integral to your work as a professional teacher. In fact, the process of questioning yourself, monitoring your teaching and monitoring your students' learning provides information you can put into your teaching portfolio.

The lecture debate

What do you want to achieve? What can you achieve? What does the literature say about what you can achieve? Before we go any further, it may be helpful to touch base with the research literature on lecturing and to acknowledge that there is, in higher education, an ongoing debate about the role of lectures as an effective learning activity. Understanding the various aspects of this debate will enable you to form your own views and think about how you can help your students learn more effectively. Even if you have very little autonomy in or control over course content, you can still learn and develop your own views.

Donald Bligh's *What's the Use of Lectures* (2001) gives an excellent and readable summary of the research on student learning from lectures and suggestions for improving your lectures. Postgraduates find this book very useful and helpful. Some of the most relevant points from his work and that of Brown (1978) are shown below.

What the research literature says about lecturing

- Students are only able to remain attentive for a maximum of 15–20 minutes, and often for only about 10 minutes. Research on student attentiveness has been repeated in many different subject areas at different levels of study and in different countries, and this is the consensus.
- There is a limit to what lectures can accomplish. All the research tells us that lectures are good for disseminating information; they are not as good as other strategies for meeting other outcomes, such as discussion, critical thinking, synthesis and evaluation, application and problem-solving.
- Strategies are needed for enhancing students' motivation to improve their attention. This is best done by stimulation, repetition, example/illustration, discussion and practice, demonstrating relevance, activities.

(Based on Bligh, 2001; Brown, 1978)

Why, then, do we spend so much time lecturing? Arguably, the reasons relate to: historical precedent ('That's what we've always done'), experience ('It's how I was taught'), comfort ('I've done my bit now and covered all those topics in the syllabus'), laziness ('It's easier to lecture than to manage a student-centred tutorial'), organisation ('That's the way the timetable is blocked out'), management ('We can only afford 1 or 2 contact hours a week') and/or ignorance ('I don't know any other way to do it').

So why are you lecturing anyway? Part of the answer may relate to one or more of these reasons we cite above. However, we would say, first, think about the learning outcomes and the assessment. Will lectures help your students to accomplish the learning outcomes? Is the teaching approach aligned? If it is, and if the main point of lecturing is to convey information that will then be assessed, then maybe the lecture is appropriate. If not, can you replace the lecture with something more suitable, such as web-based notes with a group tutorial, a student-led discussion or a library research project? If you have an opinion on this, discuss it with the module coordinator, course leader or tutor; there may be enough flexibility within the curriculum for you to make changes, and others may be open to suggestions. On the other hand, they may not.

Research says that the learning outcomes which can be met by lectures are limited (Bligh, 2001). However, the reality is that academics everywhere are under pressure to do research, generate income and teach 'efficiently', and lectures are efficient. Some departments have even decided to cut all tutorials. This means that lectures may be the only opportunity you have to interact with students and the only opportunity for students to interact with teaching staff face-to-face. Talking to 200–300 students in a lecture theatre may save money, but you will be challenged to make it effective for learning. You will have to strive hard to make the most of it.

However, there are a number of things you can do to enhance the learning outcomes from lectures. Lectures (and presentations of all sorts) are unlikely to go away, but you can improve your practice, starting with these suggestions.

How to improve your lectures

- Research – make sure you know the topic, but don't overdo it; remember that part of the research is getting information about your students and your responsibilities.
- Plan – think about what you want you and your students to accomplish and how.

- Structure – set out each part and make this transparent.
- Delivery – attend to voice, dynamics, body language.
- Visual aids – use whatever will be appropriate, interesting and exciting.
- Strategies for involvement – engage students in active learning whenever you can.

We will elaborate on each of these elements in the next sections, which deal with planning and delivering your lectures.

How do you plan?

I'm really glad I didn't write all my lecture notes over the summer because it would have been a complete waste of time ... after what you've just told me about people only concentrating for 10 minutes at a time.

I completely changed the way I taught this topic after the discussion we had about learning in lectures. The feedback was great.

What makes a good lecture? What postgraduates say to us when we ask this question is that good lectures have the following characteristics: clarity of structure; language that can be understood, and is on the right level; relevant to the subject and the course of study; interesting and engaging; stimulates thought; good delivery with respect to voice, dynamics and pace, and exhibiting confidence; good and appropriate use of resources such as diagrams, pictures, video clips, examples. These features may seem straightforward, but getting all – even most – of them right will require at least two things: planning and practice.

How do you plan for success? Before you go any further, ask yourself two questions. What is my purpose? What am I trying to do? The purpose of a lecture might be to:

- introduce a topic, give an overview or a summary;
- stimulate interest;
- present new research or topical information;
- present expert and personal knowledge;
- give a historical review;
- revise a topic or a series of topics;

- simplify complex ideas;
- structure further study.

One of the most common mistakes that postgraduates make when planning their lectures is to dive in and do lots of research and note-taking and to try and cover material that is too much for their needs and too complex. Perhaps you have already spent ages looking up information from papers and texts, even writing it all out, pages and pages of stuff 'to cover' in a lecture, just like the postgraduate speaking here:

I spent a horrendous amount of time preparing my first lecture (one morning a day for two weeks).

This is probably because you are afraid you will 'run dry' – run out of things to say before time is up. You won't. In actual fact, postgraduates never fail to be surprised by how little they can cover in 50 minutes or an hour. Put yourself in your students' place. Remember your own experiences of trying to listen and take notes during a lecture. It is hard, isn't it, to concentrate on what the lecturer is saying, write notes that will make sense later and follow the thread of the lecture? Not only will your students be trying to do several things at once but, as Bligh (2001) tells us, they will be struggling to concentrate after 15–20 minutes.

> Do not let preparing for lectures take over your life. **HEALTH WARNING**
> Most postgraduates prepare far more than they
> need to and never use all the material they have.
> Be strategic: read the rest of this chapter, think
> and plan carefully, and consider all the research and theory we've covered so
> far before you spend hours in the library.

Before you do any research and note-taking, take time to plan. Our advice is to 'keep it simple'. Focus on your purpose. Plan to cover only a few main ideas (perhaps only one to three) within an hour's session. This will allow time to flesh out those ideas, to give lots of examples or illustrations to reinforce them and build in time for students to think, discuss or practise working with them right then and there. It also means there will be time for you to repeat the key ideas, and you may have heard the old adage:

Tell them what you're going to tell them.
Tell them.
Tell them what you told them.

You may think this is a bit patronising, but the point is that you will, and should, repeat, restate or rephrase your key points so that their importance is clear and understood by students. After all, the first time you say it, some students may be having a 'micro-sleep'. Research does tell us that people do take 'time out'; that is, their attention lapses for a few seconds.

The next step is to block out your lecture, allocating time to each stage. A format is given below but, of course, you need to break down the body of your lecture into subsections. The template illustrates the relative times you might want to give to the introduction, body and conclusion – or more simply, the beginning, middle and end. In this plan, the introductory remarks require about 6 minutes, the body 36 minutes and the conclusion 8 minutes. These are obviously not fixed time allocations, but are useful as a guide. In the next few paragraphs we will discuss planning for each of the sections – introduction, main body and conclusion – and we will explain what a 'grabber' is.

Blocking out time for a one-hour lecture

6 min	Introduction: introduce yourself, mention the occasion, topic; give the 'grabber', summarise structure.
36 min	Main body: present the body of your talk.
8 min	Conclusion: summarise, take questions, look forward to next time.
50 min	Total, leaving 5 min to set up and 5 min to clear up.

First, though, after you have blocked the main parts of your lecture, you can make up a more detailed plan which will help you stay on track, remind you to 'keep it simple' and stop you doing too much. It may also force you to make decisions about what is important to keep in and what to throw out. Table 2.1 shows an example of a detailed plan. If you plan your time in this way, you can see there is actually not as much time for the body of the lecture as you first thought.

TABLE 2.1

A sample lecture plan

ACTIVITY	MINUTES
Introduction (6 min)	
Introduction, statement of aims	2
'Grabber' and summary of structure	4
Main body (36 min)	
Section A	13
Student activity A	5
Section B	13
Student activity B	5
Conclusion (8 min)	
Summary of lecture	1
Questions	5
Looking forward to the next class	1
Instructions for students	1
Total	50

Introduction

The introduction to your lecture is important because in a short time you need to do several things:

- establish credibility and rapport;
- state the aims or purpose;
- introduce main points and summarise structure;
- generate interest;
- grab student's attention – hook them.

Building rapport can be done briefly with a warm greeting, a comment about something topical and relevant to students' lives, or a reference to a common experience. As you introduce the topic of the lecture, you can establish credibility, for example, by explaining this is a particular research interest for you or by relating the topic to one of your own past experiences.

How do you generate interest, and what is a 'grabber'? This is a technique used by most good speakers to 'grab' the attention of their audience, and it works well. What techniques could you use to 'grab' the attention of your students, settle them and introduce your topic to them in an interesting and relevant way? Here are some ideas.

'Grabbing' attention

- Use your physical presence – use large gestures and a dynamic voice; if you have the confidence, be quietly dignified and just stand there silently waiting; wear interesting (but not distracting) clothing.
- Ask a rhetorical question – 'What do you think about ...?', 'Where would we find evidence for ...?', 'Why did ... happen?'
- Make a startling statement – 'Statistics on cancer death predict that ...'; quote a confrontational newspaper headline; cite a controversial quotation.
- Use a visual aid – a drawing, a cartoon, an illustration, a photograph, a diagram.

No doubt you will have ideas of your own. However, it will be necessary to fit your opening to the group; try not to use something your students will not understand or relate to or may find offensive. And your grabber should be something you feel comfortable with as well. For example, if you are not very good at telling jokes or funny stories, this may not be the technique for you.

In your introduction you should make clear the aims of the lecture (what you are trying to achieve) and you should briefly outline the structure. One way of doing this is to outline on a slide, giving the major topics, key concepts and/or sections. You can summarise the structure in a few sentences by saying, for instance, 'First I will propose a question; then we will look at two possible solutions and I will ask you to comment on the advantages and limitations of each; lastly, we will consider which of the solutions is the one of choice and why.'

Main body

Think about the best structure for what you want to do. How might you best present the ideas, concepts, key principles or debate? Is a linear structure the best approach? For example: 'There are three theoretical models to explain ... A, B and C. I am going to summarise each of these in turn, then look briefly at the limitations of each.' Perhaps you want to start with a question followed by one or more solutions: 'How do professionals deal with ...?' Or you might want to set up a compare and contrast situation. Brown (1978) explains a number of interesting approaches to structuring lectures. Whatever you do, the structure of your lecture should be explained outright so that your students know what to expect and can be thinking ahead about how to take notes.

In acknowledgement of the research, we have suggested that you should break up your lecture with some kind of activity or change of mode. There are many ideas for how you might do this and we discuss some of these below, but it will mean you are able to cover less material. Cutting down on content means, of course, that you may immediately have the problem of 'coverage', especially if the syllabus is crowded. Depending on the learning outcomes and assessment, you may find you can select out certain aspects of the material, or cover them in other ways, such as through handouts, web-based resources and/or reading assignments. Think about how else, and whether, you can cover content or simply spend time giving information. Our view is that you should spend precious contact time doing things that students cannot easily do for themselves, such as clarifying complicated concepts, stimulating learning, addressing their questions, structuring the subject matter. You cannot possibly cover all the detail anyway.

What kinds of activities can you use to engage students in active learning in a lecture theatre, possibly with large numbers of students? Postgraduates are often surprised to find out there are numerous techniques they can use to stimulate interest and attention or give students time to think, discuss or solve problems. Be creative. There are many things you can do, even in a large lecture theatre.

How to stimulate active learning in lectures

- Paired discussion – 'Turn to your neighbour and discuss the following statement.'
- Problem-solving – 'Here is a question/statement of a problem on the OHP – work on this for the next 5 minutes.'
- Watch this video clip – 'I would like you to look for these two things.'
- Listen – 'Listen to the audio tape of a child speaking and write down the words he is pronouncing.'
- Demonstration – 'Could I have a volunteer down at the front so that we can demonstrate how the scapula moves.'
- Quiz – 'Take 5 minutes to answer the four questions in this quiz. I'll project the questions onto the screen in front of you.'
- Questionnaire – 'Here's a quick questionnaire which I'd like you to complete, and then we'll have a show of hands to collate the responses.'

- True or false – 'Please answer the following four true–false questions which you can see on the overhead transparency.'
- Data analysis – 'Here are some sample data on the handout (slide). In pairs, please take 5 minutes to analyse the data using the formulae we've just been discussing. I'll take answers from some of the pairs.'
- Vote – 'Here are two points of view. Could we have a show of hands to indicate whether you agree or disagree?'

Warning: these activities will need good time management, so make sure you are not too ambitious so that you can stop them when the time is up.

Conclusion

We have all been in lectures when the speaker ran over time and did not have time for a good conclusion, or maybe even carried on as people were starting to leave. Remember that the research says it helps learning for the key message to be repeated and summarised. Furthermore, the summary will be one of the last things your students will hear you say, so it may stick in their memories. Of course, you also need to allow time for a few questions and to refer to the next lecture or tutorial so that your students will get a feel for how all this information fits together.

Finally …

For your first lecture especially, we strongly suggest you rehearse and time it, preferably in the same room where you will give your lecture. This will allow you to check the equipment that you need and give you time to make changes. If that is not possible, do check the room and equipment in advance so that you are not faced with any last-minute surprises. On the day, get there early so you can organise yourself before or as students arrive.

Doing it – what works?

Voice, body language, breathing

What are you going to do when you stand in front of the class? If you are lecturing in a very large lecture theatre, you will need to use a microphone. Make sure you know how to operate it by getting some instructions and practising first; don't stress yourself out by assuming you can cope on the day. However, regardless of whether you have a microphone, you need to think about protecting your voice. Practise standing squarely on both feet with a straight back and relax your shoulders. Your voice should arise from your diaphragm, not your throat, with breathing relaxed right down to the base of your torso. Lift your chin to project your voice to the students at the rear of the room. Listen to the pitch – the lower the better for both you and your students. Attend to the pace: breathe normally, take pauses.

People on our courses tell us that one of the things they value most highly is the sessions with a drama coach, who asks them to give a short talk to the group and then gives them personal feedback on their posture, breathing, voice, diction, speech. You might like to see if you can arrange this type of one-to-one feedback for yourself, as it will apply for all types of teaching, not just lecturing, and for all types of presentations. Typical feedback to our participants is illustrated below:

Because you're tense, your diaphragm is tight and you are breathing from the top of your chest, which raises the pitch of your voice. Breathe deeply, relax the diaphragm.

You're trying to reach the back of the room by shouting, which means you are straining your larynx. If you do this too often you will get a sore throat and lose your voice. Breathe deeply and push your speaking from the diaphragm. Lift your chin and throw the voice to the back.

You have a voice that is nice to listen to, but you let your voice fade at the ends of sentences, so sometimes we don't hear the end of the sentence.

You're rattling on like a freight train. Slow down. Pause. Pauses give your voice a rest, give students a rest from listening, and give them a chance to reflect briefly on what you've just said. Pauses can also be used for dramatic effect.

These comments illustrate some of the common problems speakers experience, but everyone can improve their presentation skills. Even if you cannot get personal tutoring or feedback, you could set up a recording and play it back to yourself.

Starting off

Having done all the research, planning, organisation and practising, you are ready to go:

- Breathe deeply, relax.
- Pause, look at your students, smile.
- Stand on both feet.
- Introduce yourself.
- Give the aims or purpose of your lecture.
- Explain your expectations of students and/or link to what came before.
- Signal the start of class, for example, by turning on the projector, then pausing.
- Explain the structure of the lecture briefly.
- Give the 'grabber'.

Observe how your students are coping with listening and writing. Are they scrabbling to get everything down on paper, or have they finished writing? Ask them to give you feedback on your voice and the pace of your talking: is it too fast or too slow? Can they all hear you? Get them working for you and with you early on.

Signposting

As you talk, continue to make the structure clear and use signposts:

- Use the introduction to frame the structure: 'First I'm going to … then … then …'.
- Indicate sections/stages as you progress: 'We've just been talking about concept A and you've had a chance to discuss the application of that. Now I'm going to move on the next section of this lecture to talk about concept B.'
- Emphasise key ideas: 'What's important here is …', 'I'd like you to remember …', 'In contrast to Bridges, Watson says …'.
- Briefly summarise each section as you move on: 'Now let's just summarise what we've been saying about A and B.'
- Use other 'signposts': 'Another aspect of this issue is …', 'Furthermore …', 'A different aspect …', 'An alternative …'.

Language and connections

You will remember that the research of Marton et al. (1997) tells us that one of the significant factors affecting learning is the knowledge and experience students already have. Remember that when you are introducing new knowledge, it has to connect with 'old' knowledge and experience. What this means is that you must be careful in your lectures to use the language that students recognise and relate to.

This means not making assumptions about what they know. Start from where they are, introducing new terms as you go and helping them to make appropriate connections. Help them make connections with the 'real world', such as the relevance of your lecture to work, leisure or other forms of study. Obviously, you want to avoid being patronising, but active dialogue with your students helps you to strike the right balance. And remember to take care that your language is inclusive, giving no hint of racism, sexism, or religious or cultural bias. If you have any doubts about this at all, tape record your lecture and listen to it carefully.

Here are some helpful dos and don'ts which apply to the kind of language you use.

Dos and don'ts

Do

- Use short sentences.
- Compare with similes and metaphors.
- Link with experience.
- Use stories and examples.
- Provide breaks and pauses.
- Be true to yourself.

Don't

- Use clichés: 'Until the cows come home.'
- Use jargon: 'You can download sites from hot links straight onto your memory stick through the USB port.'
- Use absolute language: 'never', 'always', 'forever'.
- Use sexist language: 'Women will understand …', or the generic 'he' to refer to all.

Stimulating interest and active learning

In the earlier section on planning, we offered ideas for stimulating interest and motivation, involving students in activities and helping students to learn. The list below gives more examples, followed by useful tips.

Techniques for helping students to learn

- Use visual aids: overhead projector (OHP), PowerPoint, slides, photographs, video clips, diagrams, flowcharts, sound recordings, links to the web.
- Use graphics where you can for statistical/technical data.
- Use case studies, examples, personal experience to show relevance.
- Show links to seminars, workshops, labs, clinical situations.
- Illustrate with images: use visual aids, pictures, diagrams, charts.
- Organise activities, such as those given earlier: questions, problem-solving, case study, quiz.

Overhead projector   The rule of thumb here is again to 'keep it simple'. Use a type size and font that will be easily readable to all – commonly Times Roman or Arial type and font size 24 or larger. If you use very large font, it will automatically restrict how many words you can fit onto the transparency, and this is not a bad thing. Use black, dark blue or dark green; reds, oranges and pale colours are difficult to read.

PowerPoint   Although PowerPoint is not very old, it is already being overused (in our view) and students are beginning to suffer PowerPoint fatigue – especially since most people use the bullet-point format for their presentations. The format you use for your PowerPoint slides may vary. Some institutions may insist on corporate templates, others allow you to choose. Whatever, the template should be simple so as not to distract from the content. Use either dark text on a white or plain, pale background, or white or pale colour type on a plain, dark background. Recommended colour combinations are blue or black with white or pale yellow. Type sizes and fonts are the same as those recommended above for overhead transparencies.

A big advantage of PowerPoint is the capacity to incorporate digital photographs, diagrams, charts and graphs, and to use web-based resources, linking directly to websites through 'hot links'. A disadvantage is some lack of flexibility, making it more difficult to go back to a slide or revisit a point, for example, if a student asks a question or wants further clarification of a point you made previously.

Video   This is a very good way to demonstrate application and to show relevance in real life, such as the workplace. Your video can focus on a case study, a scenario, personal opinion, examples, illustrations. It is a good idea to give students, in advance, something specific to look for, unless you are just wanting a general response. It is also a good idea to restrict video clips to about 5 minutes, otherwise students go into 'cinema mode', especially if the room is dark and warm, and their attention span drops.

Slides, photographs and diagrams   These are perfect tools for teaching most subjects, although you will need to organise them in advance, and make sure the technology is there to project the images. If you are using diagrams that students will need to know a lot about later, such as anatomical or engineering diagrams, it is a very good idea to give them photocopies or put them on the web so they can access them later.

Audio tape   Make sure you will have the proper equipment to play the tape and project the sound so that everyone can hear it.

Flipcharts, whiteboard and blackboard   Do not rule out these tools for lectures. Although flipcharts cannot be seen from the back of a large lecture hall, they are suitable for smaller venues. You will need to write large enough for students to read. You may also use the whiteboard or blackboard to good effect, providing you write legibly and with large lettering. In fact, writing serves to slow you down and allows students to 'catch up', so it can be a useful technique.

Modelling thinking   This can be a really good way to demonstrate how you think through a problem, for example in maths or physics, or how you collect information or evidence to inform choices. Scribbling thoughts as a mind map or spontaneous diagram on the whiteboard can draw students into this process as well.

Handouts   Some academics give students a full transcript of their lectures. We would discourage this for several reasons, including the photocopy costs you will accumulate. A better solution is to give students a partial handout containing main headings, complicated diagrams or data, but with gaps where they can fill in their own notes. Of course, miniature PowerPoint slides or outlines can be printed to help students with note-taking, but these may not suit students with dyslexia or sight disabilities, and complex diagrams will be almost impossible for anyone to read.

Note-taking   Help students with note-taking. You can be explicit about what you think they should write down, for example, 'Take a few minutes to write this statement down in your notes' (then shut up and let them write!) or 'You have the handout, so just put down your pens and listen for now.' Stop talking now and then so that students can catch up.

Making connections between lectures   Refer back to a previous lecture or refer forward to a future occasion. Refer to laboratory or fieldwork or to a tutorial. Even better, refer to something they may be studying in another module.

Getting students to speak up and ask questions in lectures   One of the things that often worries postgraduates is how to get students involved. It is common for new lecturers to try and get students to participate by asking questions, either of the group as a whole or of individual students. In our experience, that approach can be stressful for students. How do you feel when you are asked to answer a direct question in the presence of a large group of people? Certainly, for young students, this can be an intimidating experience, exposing their intellectual attributes.

A more constructive, and easier, approach to engaging students is to create short tasks for them to do in the lecture. Not only does this get everyone involved, instead of just one person, but it means you can direct what happens. You can tell them exactly what you would like them to do, step by step, and how they should report the results of that activity. Students feel safer because they know what they are to do, they have time to think about the task and organise answers, and they can share the answers with each other. So no one feels exposed. One of the first activities you might give them is to discuss, in pairs, their answers to a question you set them or their answers to a questionnaire that you project onto the screen. Getting pairs of students to talk to each other is a failsafe strategy, even for first-year students who are often the most reluctant to speak up. All of the activities that we suggest in this and the previous section will tempt students to talk, especially if they work, initially at least, in pairs or threes. But the task must be structured and your instructions clear; otherwise they may start to talk about other things, such as shopping, food or dating.

Conclusion

You have done well, and you are nearly there. Keep an eye on the clock so that you have sufficient time to draw your lecture to a conclusion, summarise the key points and take a few questions. Make a connection between your lecture and what the students will be doing next, in the next lecture, tutorial or practical session. Finish with a sense of completion. Congratulate yourself for doing it well. Go for a break and relax.

Postgraduate fears

Even when postgraduates have prepared well, they still have fears. Postgraduates who talk to us about starting teaching tell us these are the things they most worry about:

- Answering questions: 'What do I do if I can't answer a question?'
- Don't know enough: 'I just feel like I don't know enough to be teaching this subject at this level', 'I worry I won't be seen to have enough credibility in the subject.'
- Drying up: 'I'm so nervous. I'm afraid the stage fright will dry up my mouth, make my hands tremble uncontrollably, and everyone will know I'm scared.'
- Losing the thread of your narrative: 'When I'm nervous, I sometimes just lose the plot.'
- Omitting important facts: 'What if I forget to tell them something important?'
- Equipment failure: 'What do I do if the computer crashes or the overhead projector blows a bulb?'
- Questions which interrupt: 'I don't think I could handle questions that interrupt my talk. I'd lose track of where I was and my timing would get messed up.'
- Noisy or badly behaved students: 'What do I do if the students are noisy or unruly? How should I handle that?'
- Students look bored: 'I think I'll just fold up if I look out at the sea of faces, and they all look bored to death.'

The fear of not being able to answer a question or command the respect of students may be why so many postgraduates overprepare for lectures. Most people who are new to lecturing do overinvest for fear they will not know enough or will not have enough material. For postgraduates, this might sometimes be to the detriment of their research. Remember that you cannot and do not need to cover everything. You are there to provide structure, to guide and stimulate thinking, to present basic ideas and principles and to introduce new concepts. Don't overreach; don't overinvest. Invest time in finding reinforcing material, examples and illustrations rather than in cramming in more facts which students probably will not remember anyway.

Dealing with questions has a lot to do with confidence. First, tell yourself you know more than all or nearly all your students, or you would not be where you are now. Second, if you are asked a question you cannot answer, say so. Do not try to bluff your way out, because you will almost certainly paint yourself into a corner, and the bluff will be obvious anyway. However, if you have some knowledge of the question or of a similar situation or circumstance or research, you could talk about this, indicating that this is related information. So your answer might be, 'Well I don't know about this specific situation, but in a similar case … .' You might also ask if anyone else knows the answer. If they do, thank them for their contribution. If they do not, and you think it is an important or interesting question, suggest that they might search for an answer, giving one or two sources as a starting point. If you think an answer is important to help student understanding, either offer to look it up for next time or tell the students where they are likely to find an answer.

Drying up, losing the thread and forgetting facts most commonly happen when people are nervous or anxious. One way to deal with anxiety is to prepare well. If you have planned your lecture carefully, know what you are going to say and do, have notes and materials organised, you will find you are much less worried. Additionally, because you have done all the preliminary work, you can concentrate on the delivery – the here and now – and you will be more confident. If you think your mouth might get dry, take water with you. If you lose the thread, just stop and say, 'Now where was I?' and look at your notes. If you forget something altogether, ask yourself if it is really that important. If it is, deal with it next time, send an email or post a message on the web for students.

Equipment failures sometimes happen, but there are ways to deal with them. If you get caught out, you may need to persevere, using the whiteboard or blackboard to jot a few key notes. Do not stop the class and leave the room to look for a spare bulb or an IT support person. However, if you are using PowerPoint and worry about the equipment, take transparencies with you, just in case. If you are using the overhead projector, there is usually a spare bulb, and you need to learn how to switch it over. Some (not many) lecturers even carry spare bulbs with them. If you have prepared handouts, just talk to those. Students, on the whole, would rather you just get on with it; after all, it is their time too.

Some lecturers like to take questions in the middle of their lectures, as it allows them to address issues then and there, before they move onto a new topic. Others prefer to deal with them at the end. This is really up to you and you should do what you are comfortable with, certainly in the beginning. Tell your students which approach you will be using. If they do not all get to ask their questions, ask them to write them down and give them to you before they leave or to email you.

In fact, if you are worried about dealing with questions during lectures, this might be your best option.

What do you do about noisy or unruly students? In our experience this does not often happen, and in fact, usually students are too quiet. You can frequently circumvent problems from the beginning by asking students to agree to some ground rules during your first introduction. This can be done politely and quickly; then if students subsequently become too disruptive, you can refer back to the ground rules they agreed to. If they persist in disrupting the class, ask yourself why. Are they bored? Have they heard all this already? Is the material over their heads? Is it late in the day when they are tired? You may even need to speak to some of them to get answers to your questions, but that could be quite helpful. If you find you still have problems dealing with the situation, speak to your module coordinator or course leader and ask for help.

Lastly, what if some students look as though they are bored? First of all, do not assume they are; they may actually be listening. Second, if you have tried to involve them in some form of active learning, they will be much less likely to be disengaged. Third, if you have tried hard, try to get some feedback from them to understand what the problem might be; perhaps it is their fifth lecture in one day. Fourth, do not be disheartened; you cannot possibly be all things to all people all the time.

Measuring the learning and getting feedback on your teaching

You should be thinking about collecting feedback on two things: your students' learning and your teaching. As we mentioned in the first part of this chapter, there is a lively debate in higher education about the value of lectures for learning. Therefore, getting feedback from students in lectures on what they are learning and how you are teaching should be part of what you do. This feedback can then help you think about how you might continue to enhance their learning by changing what you do. We cover feedback much more extensively in Chapter 10, but here are some quick and useful techniques for you to think about now.

Feedback on learning

Overhead quizzes   Put a few questions on an overhead transparency or onto a PowerPoint slide. Number them so that students can simply write down the numbers on a slip of paper, put their answers next to them, and pass them to the end of the row for collection. You can do a quick survey to see if students are understanding what you hoped they would.

The one-minute paper (Angelo and Cross, 1993)   This is a quick way to find out what students understand from your lectures (see also Chapter 10). Again, on a projected slide, ask two questions:

1   In your own words, what is (are) the key point(s) of today's lecture?
2   What question still remains unclear (unresolved) for you?

This technique can be varied according to what it is you want to know. Perhaps you want to know if students can transfer a principle or theory to another context, so your question could be:

- How would this theory apply to the following situation? (Then give a simple brief.)
- How does the theory we have just discussed differ from that proposed by Paul Green of The New University?

Post-it questions   Give students one or more Post-its and ask them to give you their comments in response to prompts, such as 'learned', 'need to know more about', 'don't understand'. This technique has also been described in Chapter 1.

Feedback on teaching

Overhead questionnaire   Put a few questions on a slide. Ask students to give the number of each question and their responses on a piece of paper. The types of questions you might ask would be:

- What do you like best about my lectures?
- What do you like least about my lectures?
- How do my lectures help you to learn the subject?
- How do they not help you to learn the subject?
- What do you like best/least about the way I lecture?

Post-it feedback   As above, ask students to take three Post-its, but the headers might be 'stop', 'start' and 'continue'. That is, what should I stop doing, what should I start to do and what should I continue with?

Note/letter/advice to a friend   Ask students to write a brief note to a friend about what they like or do not like about your lectures – anonymously, of course. This kind of feedback can be very powerful and useful.

Portfolio

When you start your lecturing is an ideal time to collect materials for your portfolio and document the lecturing process. You might include each of your lecture plans, plus 100 words for each plan about why you chose to do it that way, what you wanted to accomplish and how it went in general.

Your commentary could include examples of interactive activities with some reflective comment about how well they went – how enthusiastic students seemed, whether they arrived at the conclusions you expected or not, and whether the activities seemed to integrate well with your lecture. If you built in some form of evaluation of an activity, as we suggest above, you could put the results in here too.

Keeping teaching notes or a teaching journal is one way to monitor your work. Or you may want to devise a simple pro forma which you fill in after each lecture: what went well and why; what didn't go well and why; what you would do differently. Other questions you could ask yourself might be, for example, how do you know you are covering the right things? How do you monitor that, and what evidence can you provide? What topics do students find easy or difficult, and why do you think that is? Reviewed retrospectively, these notes can be really useful starting points for your portfolio.

More importantly, you can begin to think ahead. What are the implications of your experience (and student evaluations) for your future teaching? What questions remain – about what does and does not work and why – and how will you set about finding answers to them?

Additional resources

Bligh, D. (2001) *What's the Use of Lectures?* Exeter: Intellect.
Many of our postgraduates and new lecturers love this book for its comprehensive coverage of the research literature on learning from lectures and clear presentation of so many useful ideas for improving lectures.

3

Your First Tutorials

Experienced staff in my department tell me that students don't do the reading and won't talk in tutorials. How am I going to overcome that if they can't?

If you think about your own learning: how much of that has been when you have been in a group situation? Learning through group work happens all the time, and not just in academic courses, but also in other contexts.

Within academic institutions, historically, tutorials have been a major part of learning and teaching strategies. More recently, postgraduates have been given more responsibility for tutorials. Therefore, this is almost certainly a teaching activity for which you will be responsible.

This chapter summarises the key principles and strategies for running tutorials and seminars. We cover what you need to know to get through your first semester, without any major disasters and without too much stress.

If this seems to be a longer chapter than the others, that is because it is. The reason for this is that postgraduates tell us they feel most vulnerable or 'on the spot' when they are running a tutorial. When you work with a small group, there is no hiding place. Of course, many tutorials these days are not 'small groups' at all – some are quite large – but the fact remains that postgraduates still find tutorials testing. This may be because you are still developing the skills of managing groups. You will also need strategies for dealing with, potentially, an increased level of interaction with students.

Tutorials can be extremely rewarding learning experiences for your students, if they are handled well. To help you achieve this, we provide a bit of background on tutorials – some definitions, theory and key principles you need to make them run well – and we suggest other useful material. Perhaps more importantly, we deal with the practical aspects of group work, including the importance of planning and developing skills, and we propose options for activities you can run in your groups. We work through a list of problems that postgraduates often tell us about, offering solutions. Finally, we make suggestions for your teaching portfolio and suggest additional sources of information to help you with group teaching.

What is the purpose of tutorials?

What is a tutorial? What is it for? If you were to ask different people, you would get different definitions, but it is probably safe to say that, generally understood, tutorials are there to help your students develop their understanding of the subject matter through discussion and group activity.

There are many variations on this theme. For example, a tutorial could be students working in groups of three or four to discuss a case scenario, problem, data set or experiment. Or it could be a larger group of students watching a video, followed by tutor-led discussion. Or it could be what is more commonly referred to as a seminar, which is generally understood to mean students critically appraising academic materials.

In the examples given above, students might be involved in discussion, problem-solving, analysing, summarising and evaluating. Clearly, these activities are not just about understanding the subject matter. What else might students be developing? What do you think group learning can accomplish? Table 3.1 lists six different aims of group learning and suggests how they can be achieved through specific activities. This list suggests that group work is not just about getting your students to understand the subject area. Learning about the subject matter – or consolidating their learning – is, of course, crucial, but group work provides valuable opportunities for your students to develop other skills, both as group members and as learners.

You may hear the term 'skills' used in discussions in your department. For example, 'communication' is sometimes referred to as a 'soft skill', perhaps implying that it is marginal to the 'hard' learning of academic subjects. However, if your students are to demonstrate their knowledge and use it in some way in group work, effective communication skills, such as those detailed below, are central. Other skills are important for learning too, so you may have to help your students to progress more than one of the aims in the table.

Consideration of the complexity of group processes, and of the importance of 'skills' in academic courses, reveals a focus on the tutor. How often do we share discussions about the purpose of group learning with students? Do we tell them what our intentions are? How do we check that they have understood what we mean by our terms, aims and outcomes? If you reflect on your own experience, how were you briefed on the goals of group work as a student?

TABLE 3.1

Typical aims of group learning (based on Forster, 1995)

AIMS	EXAMPLES
1 Understanding Helping students to consolidate their understanding	Clarifying concepts Reflecting on connections Testing understanding through examples, cases, illustrations
2 Critical thinking Helping students to develop capacity for thinking critically	Reviewing evidence in light of theory Learning to set and solve problems or approach issues and questions Logical reasoning and argument
3 Personal growth Helping students to develop as individuals	Clarifying attitudes and values Developing confidence and self-esteem Responsibility and commitment
4 Communication skills Helping students to learn how to communicate with others	Refining, listening, questioning, explaining Presenting and defending a position Giving and receiving feedback
5 Group and team skills Helping students to learn how to collaborate and work as a team	Setting, allocating and monitoring tasks Supporting others in the group Initiating, directing and leading tasks
6 Self-direction in learning	Clarifying own learning goals Managing study time and effort Prioritising Taking responsibility for evaluating progress as learners

In practice, we probably only rarely – that is, not as often as we should – take the time to discuss this with students. Sometimes we might say, 'This is to help you understand the lectures', but we may not routinely go into all the other stuff. We may not explain that the tutorials are meant to enhance skills for high level thinking, learning, group work and personal development.

How will you articulate your selection of these aims – and/or others – for a specific tutorial to your students? You may find that taking time at the beginning to discuss this with your students will mean they are more willing to participate actively in group work because they understand what it is for. Because terms like those in Table 3.1 are likely to appear in course or module descriptors, there is all the more reason to discuss them with your students. If you find it useful and more meaningful to students to use different terms to get the point across, how will you make the link back to the more formal language for the purposes of your portfolio, quality assurance and enhancement, and so on?

How do groups work?

Most people experience two kinds of groups, social groups and task groups:

- In social groups, success is measured in terms of how enjoyable the group work is.
- In task groups, success is measured in terms of the work the group gets done.

Many groups are a mixture of the two.

In practice, for your student groups to work well, they will need both dimensions: the social dimension to stimulate students' emotional involvement, to build morale and loyalty, and the task dimension to create stability, focus, purpose, direction and a sense of achievement (Jacques, 2000). You therefore need to think about both dimensions as you plan and prepare yourself and your students for group processes and tasks. This is not to say that you will be forming a 'social' group in your tutorials; instead, it means that part of your role as tutor is to establish a positive environment to ensure that there is a social dimension.

Once people are in a group, you will know from experience that they can take on different roles. You can observe these roles in your groups as they are working. Listed below is a variety of roles and responsibilities for the two types of group.

Group roles and responsibilities

Task functions

- Initiating – starting discussion/moving to new topic – 'The topic today is …', 'Perhaps a good place to start would be …'.
- Information seeking – 'What have we got so far …?'
- Diagnosing – 'Have we gone off the track …?'
- Opinion-seeking – 'What do you think …?'
- Evaluating – 'Have we got all we need …?', 'Does this help us answer the question …?', 'Should we now …?'
- Decision-making – 'Let's stop there and …', 'I think we need to …', 'Let's move on to …'.

Maintenance or social functions

- Encouraging – praise/thanks for a comment – 'That's a great idea ...', 'That will help us with ...'.
- Compromising – 'We can use both of those to ...'.
- Peace-keeping – humour/consensus/dialogue – 'These different views show two ways forward.'
- Clarifying/summarising – 'Can you explain ...?'
- Standard-setting – 'The task requires ...', 'We need more on/of ...', 'The criteria require us to ...'.

(Adapted from Jacques, 2000: 28–9)

For your groups to be productive, your students should be taking on these responsibilities. However, it might be productive to discuss roles with them, considering what each might involve, possibly observing and reviewing how they are manifested during group work. To help you, a fuller discussion of group roles and responsibilities can be found in Jacques (2000).

Usually people take these roles 'naturally'. You might also find that the roles shift, even within the same group session. Someone may be an opinion-seeker and then take on a compromising role. The point is that students need to be aware that this is happening and is a 'normal', if not essential, part of group dynamics. It will help them to have a better understanding of group processes. Therefore, one of your roles as tutor is to coach your students as you go along. You will have to allocate time for this however.

There are, of course, roles that impact negatively on groups: blocking, aggressing, seeking recognition, special pleading, withdrawing and dominating (Jacques, 2000: 29). People who exhibit such behaviour can affect both the social and the task dimensions of the group, creating bad feelings and hindering progress towards completion of the task. Your students need to know about this and you need to know how to deal with it; we come back to this issue towards the end of this chapter.

If you think about your own experience of working in groups, you will realise that groups are dynamic organisms; they are constantly moving. This movement affects and is affected by the relationships between the people in the group and the processes, and it can impact on the group's productivity. The key point for you to remember is that there are many variables which contribute to the group dynamics: this is why group work is complex. Your job is to ensure that your student groups run as smoothly as possible and that any shifts in dynamics are not so big that they jeopardise the work. This is why planning is so important: when you walk into the classroom, you need to know exactly what you and your students are going to do, so that you can concentrate on making it happen.

These are the main factors that may affect the dynamics operating within your tutorial group:

- commonality of purpose;
- the interest and commitment of each participant to the aims of the group;
- the relationship of members within the context of the group;
- interaction of individual personalities;
- personal agendas;
- level of participation;
- shared knowledge;
- degree of cooperation;
- group size;
- setting and physical environment.

For example, take 'level of participation'. You might have a mixed group of students – mature and younger – where the mature students are happy to talk, and the younger students are happy to let them. However, the willingness to talk may not be so cut-and-dried. It may not just be about their age; it might also be about their subject knowledge and their experience of working in groups; or it may be because the mature students know each other.

As leader of the group you have to take into consideration that all of this is happening in your tutorials. If you are to be successful in facilitating group work, you need to appreciate that these factors – not just your performance as tutor – may be shaping what happens in the group. In addition, to be an effective group leader you must be constantly observing and reacting to the behaviours of individuals during your group activity. If you see, as you scan your group or eavesdrop, that a group is not working or that individuals in a group are tuning out, then you will be able to step into the appropriate role to bring it back on track.

Even when you are monitoring, groups can go wrong, so that students become distressed by what has happened. In some cases, and in our own experience, the cause may be that the tutor simply forgot to establish ground rules with the group. Because students work fairly often in groups, it is easy for tutors to make the assumption that they do not need to go over ground rules yet again, or that they can cover them quickly, so as to get them started on the task. The ground rule might be something simple, like not personalising criticism. Once the ground rule is broken, you have to step in quickly. Otherwise, the group process can

TABLE 3.2

Relationship between group size, purpose and student learning

GROUP SIZE	SUITED TO	STUDENT LEARNING
Pairs/threes	Generating data Checking data Sharing interpretations	Communication skills Clarifying Cooperation Group commitment grows Growing sense of safety in group Confidence through involvement Participation for all
Fours/tens	Generating ideas Criticising ideas Multiple role tasks Wide range of tasks	Dealing with decreased safety Channelling enthusiasm Creating group cohesion Using multiple resources in group
More than ten	Wide-ranging tasks Open-ended tasks Presentations	Creating supportive climate Dealing with dominance Relating to leaders Managing subgroups and divisions

become destructive. It could be argued that the simple, obvious step of establishing ground rules is one of your most important tasks.

If it all goes wrong, do not just run away. Take the next session to review what happened. Ask 'Why?' in order to learn from the answers. This is why group learning can be so powerful; it raises issues about how people situate themselves socially, about their personalities, about how they relate to other people and so on, during the course of their studies. Malfunction and meltdown may be every new tutor's fears – along with the horror of group silence – but perhaps these result more often from lack of planning than from lack of experience.

Another factor affecting the dynamics of your groups will be the size of each group, but you can design group work so that, depending on the task, size fits function (Forster, 1995). Table 3.2 illustrates how you can use tasks which are suitable to group size, and also gives examples of typical outcomes for student learning.

What this model tells us is that as the group size increases, student experience of the safety and effectiveness of group work decreases. The optimal size of groups – depending on what you want to do – is either pairs/threes or fours/sixes. With larger groups – more than 10 – subgroups will form, and it becomes more difficult to plan. Focus on the task can easily be lost.

Of course, students can also do work on their own in your tutorials. The individual has limited resources, but individual work is suited to personal reflection and generating personal data. Typical outcomes for individual student learning are building on prior learning, commitment to study and latitude for personal development.

Your best starting point may be to use the first tutorial to get to know your students. Pairs or threes will work well for this step, as they are very good for sharing ideas and interpretations, practising communication skills and getting to know each other.

- What have they done before?
- What do they remember from previous courses?
- Can they make connections with previous and other ongoing courses?
- What are their existing discussion skills like?

This act of allowing time for students to get to know each other – for socialising – is crucial for both you and your students. It also gives you – and them – valuable information about who is in the group. If you miss out this step, you may have the unpleasant experience of pitching your first tutorial at the wrong level or in the wrong tone, and then it can be very difficult to win them back:

I made the incorrect assumption that all my students would have been trained in a certain approach. Some had, but others hadn't. This made discussion difficult. Next time I would find out who had done what and maybe get those who had been trained to work with those who hadn't. Or I might keep the two groups separate.

Checking your students' starting point should stop you making some false assumptions. You can also use this discussion to prompt them to make some connections between the classes they have attended or are attending now and the sequence of tutorials you are about to start. Perhaps more importantly, it may be that the students themselves see that there are different perspectives and starting points in the tutorial group.

The point of this section is that it helps if you understand something about how groups work before you plan your tutorials. We cannot overemphasise how important it is to plan group learning carefully to ensure your students gain maximum benefit.

Planning

Structuring group work

This section makes the case that you cannot just walk into a tutorial, set a group task and leave your students to get on with it. Nor can you facilitate a group discussion by 'winging it'. Even if you have been given materials, resources and a template for the tutorial, you still have to do some preparation. Planning, in the context of group work, means planning not only the task – in terms of learning outcomes – but also the student interactions.

What are the learning outcomes? Think in detail about exactly what your students will do, how they will report back, how long everything will take, how you will draw everything together at the end, to make sure that your students understand what's been achieved. Unlike in lectures, where you do all the work, in tutorials the students are doing most of the work. Timing is critical. You need to allocate enough time for students to do every stage of the work, including summarising their learning.

Planning for group work involves you working through all the elements – thinking through the options available – and making coherent choices. The following guidelines for planning group-based learning will help you think about the details ahead of time so that you don't miss anything.

Check venue and environment   Check that the venue is suitable in terms of physical facilities. If there are difficulties with the room that you cannot change, at least you can make adjustments if you are already prepared.

State aims and outcomes   Make sure that students will understand: the aims of the session; how they connect with the rest of the programme; and what they can expect from the session.

Establish ground rules   Plan to discuss and agree with students: how they should prepare; norms of behaviour; and the roles of tutor and students.

Plan tasks   Design tasks which: are appropriate to the aims and outcomes of the session(s); will involve students in active learning; will be motivating; and are preceded by clear instructions (e.g. when a rapporteur is to make a presentation).

Structure and sequence tasks   Ensure that: tasks early in the session(s) involve everyone; outcomes from one task lead into another; and time allocations for tasks are set and kept. Try to be realistic about time allocations; they almost always take more time than you think.

Activities for group work

Remember, as we discussed in Chapter 1, it is 'what the student does' that is important for their learning (Biggs, 2003). What exactly are your students going to do in your tutorials? What follows is not an exhaustive list, and all the techniques listed can be tailored and tweaked to suit your objectives, but the main types of activity are here. This should be enough for your first semester. For further discussion and examples, see Habeshaw et al. (1984), Jacques (2000) and Knight (2002).

Guided discussion   Students ask questions or make comments, or tutor asks questions of students. Tutor led/directed. Works well in a large or small group. Useful for modelling thinking, problem-solving, critical analysis.

Step-by-step discussion   Discussion is structured around pre-prepared text, audio or video material. Suitable for critical observation, analysis, critique, problem-solving.

Buzz groups   Students in a large group or a lecture are requested to discuss a question or situation briefly (for example, for two minutes) with one or two other students. Then students feed back their responses. Useful for generating and sharing ideas, stimulating communication, starting off a tutorial.

Cascading   Students are given a task to work on or a question to discuss in pairs. They then work in fours, then move from fours into eights, and so on, until a suitable point is reached to report back to the main group. At each stage the initial task can be refined. Works well for summarising and prioritising.

Crossover groups   This is an alternative to plenary reports from groups: instead of reporting back to the whole group, students progress to a new group and report on what happened in their former group before discussion continues. Students have responsibility for reporting to their new group what happened in their previous group. Gives each student responsibility for participating, understanding and communicating the information from the first group. Does require tight organisation and enough people to make it work.

Problem-solving   This provides opportunities for students to work collaboratively on a challenging question or task. Careful thought needs to be given to structuring the task. Can be used in many contexts and situations.

Case studies   Students are presented with case notes or scenarios (in advance) and asked to produce an analysis of the situation and/or a solution to the problem presented. Can include elements of role-play but this is not essential. Excellent technique for developing subject-related and professional skills and for demonstrating 'real-world' relevance.

Peer tutoring Students teach each other. There are many ways in which students can play the role of tutor in small groups and seminars. Useful for consolidating and deepening understanding, and works for any size of group.

Projects These are extended problem-solving activities pursued cooperatively by teams of students. Develops many cognitive and transferable skills.

Games and simulations These can be fun, but need a clear purpose, in terms of the learning process. Students will be familiar with a range of formats and options from TV and radio that can be adopted or adapted. Can be motivating and based on authentic scenarios.

Role-play Structured activity allows students to explore, for example, different perspectives and relationships. Can be scripted and unscripted. Supports development of personal transferable skills and attitudes but needs careful management and good ground rules.

Brainstorming Students (usually the whole group) contribute orally any ideas they have on a subject. Ideas are recorded (flipchart or board) without comment. All ideas are recorded without selection or interpretation. Useful for generating ideas and discussion and stimulating discussion. Works well in large groups and lectures.

Whichever strategy you choose, plan exactly what your students are to do next, and how they report back (orally, posters, overheads, Post-its). Write clear and detailed instructions, including the questions they are to answer and, always, how much time they have for each activity. Even if your oral explanations are crystal clear, a written statement provides a useful focus for the group and will help them remember what to do.

Sample plan for your first tutorial

10 min   Introduce yourself.
          Put the students into pairs and get them to introduce and say
          something about themselves.

10 min	Explain the purpose and format of tutorials.
	Deal with administrative duties (register, venue, timetable, syllabus).
	Discuss ground rules.
	Stress your role as facilitator, their roles as participators.
	Give aims and outcomes.
15 min	Ask pairs to work together and give them a task: a specific topic or question to discuss, a problem to solve, a scenario, etc. Explain how you want them to report back and what you are looking for.
10 min	Move to a general discussion.
	Note/flipchart their answers to the question set. Prompt them to comment on similarities and differences.
	If they are reluctant to talk, ask them to write down their observations and get them talking in pairs, perhaps with new partners.
5 min	Summarise what they said. Praise good comments. Correct errors?
5 min	Explain what they will need to do for next time.

Pairing people up never fails, in the sense that it helps them get to know each other, generates discussion right from the start, and gives every participant a way of expressing their view (at least in writing, if not in speaking, for all of them). Most importantly for this first session, it gives you important insights not only into what they know, but how they work in groups. It is best at this stage to keep things fairly simple and straightforward. Of course, you will not use exactly this structure for all of your tutorials. You will have different aims, and therefore different tasks and timings, for future meetings. However, you should probably have stated aims, defined timings and tasks, and appropriate group strategies for those tasks for your first semester, and arguably thereafter. It might help your students to know what is expected of them if you shared all this with them.

Our postgraduates say that what they worry about is being in front of their class on the first day: 'I'm terrified.' We will discuss the skills that can smooth the way for you and help give you confidence. However, because you need similar skills for all kinds of group facilitation, we first talk a bit about seminars.

Seminars

What is a seminar? It is usually where students critique academic material. The format is often students sitting around a boardroom-type table presenting a paper, while other students listen, and the listeners are charged with asking questions after the presentation.

In our experience, this is difficult to manage, can be boring and probably results in only one person reading the paper carefully. It is not the best formula for stimulating students to engage with the reading material or to be deeply involved in the group activity. That may be why, as is often informally reported, 'students will not read the material'.

In reality, you may find that some of your students have read the material, but were not confident about discussing their views in this format. Some may even struggle to formulate a view on the reading. Some will find it difficult to come up with immediate responses to the student paper. Reticence, lack of confidence and lack of oral skills can, in other words, all be interpreted – or misinterpreted – as lack of application to the readings. Giving students a paper to read or a question to consider in advance may help them to participate – and thereby learn to state and modulate their views – but there will always be some students who find the subject so complex or the seminar format so intimidating that they stay silent.

If this is true, and if we assume that some students will struggle in these ways, then part of a tutor's role is to help students to develop these skills. You can use the techniques covered in this chapter to help them to feel safe in stating a view. You can give positive feedback to encourage further contributions. Best of all, you can motivate your students to become involved in seminar debates.

You can try to get students involved by minimising, or defining, the task:

- Define the volume of reading they have to do, the number of hours they will have to allocate to the task, the writing activities that will help them understand what they are reading and prepare to talk about it.
- Define the stages in the task, suggesting more than one way in which they can perform it.
- Lower the level: define criteria in terms of what would be 'good enough'.
- Prompt them to share the load, to carve up the preparation tasks among a subgroup.
- 'Walk' them through the task, answering their questions along the way.

If that seems to be underselling the seminar or encouraging your students to cut corners – or spelling out the obvious – you do not need to do this all at the start or with all your groups. This raises the question of how you will know how much coaching in seminar techniques they will need.

In order to find this out, it might help you – and your students – to work through a set task during your first seminar. For example, you might set up a structured discussion or debate, where students make the case for different answers to a question or different solutions to a problem.

As with other forms of teaching covered in this book, the point is not just to get through the content for that day. As a tutor your role includes helping your students to find ways to learn in this format. Some will be quite ready to do that; others will need more help. Perhaps the trickiest part of the tutor's role is catering to these different levels of skill.

This is perhaps the most complex form of teaching. Only take this on if you have developed the skills, knowledge and confidence for managing seminar groups. 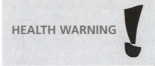 **HEALTH WARNING**

Facilitation skills

How many functions do facilitators perform during group learning? As we said earlier in the chapter, this is a complex situation, often challenging, but highly rewarding when it goes well. Here, in brief, are the key skills you will need to get started.

Listen   Attend to what is said by each person in the group. Show a readiness to actively listen through your verbal responses, eye contact and body language. How will you do that?

Question   Use a variety of questioning strategies (for example, open, closed and reflective questions). Use questioning strategies sensitively and flexibly. Think, in advance, about the kinds of questions you might ask (see below).

Explain and clarify   Try to be succinct. Build students' ideas into your explanations, when possible. Remember to connect with what they already know. Remember not to turn the tutorial into a mini-lecture.

Encourage participation   Encourage everyone to contribute and to talk to each other. Facilitate rather than dominate. Intervene appropriately (for example, to restrain, encourage, defuse, refocus). Establish a congenial atmosphere in which everyone's opinions and experiences are acknowledged. Allocate responsibilities, such as leader, secretary/scribe, timekeeper and rapporteur, and rotate these around during the semester.

Respond to students as individuals   Address students by their preferred names. Show sensitivity to students as individuals (i.e. taking into account their backgrounds and prior knowledge). Give constructive feedback.

Close   Discuss what has been achieved, what are the next steps, what are the links to the curriculum/lectures etc.

Monitor and evaluate   Make opportunities for the group to review the process. Evaluate the quality of work produced by individuals within the group or by the group as a whole. Make links with the course assessment. Check that everyone knows how they are being assessed in your tutorials, if they are.

Provide grounding   Making connections between different elements of the course is an important subject in itself and could feature as a discussion topic, at least from time to time, at the end of group activities. Alternatively, you can start a tutorial with a review – by the students – of what they have done so far in lectures, reading and other activities: what's been covered in the lectures?

Time management   Keep the group to time. It may seem obvious to say 'ensure that time allocations for tasks are set and kept', but you will find that group tasks almost always take longer than you think. For your students, time may pass more quickly than they are aware. It is up to you to make sure that they get through it all. Although this is a simple point, it takes a bit of thought and plenty of observation on your part to do this well. It isn't easy.

Monitor attendance   If you have students who simply do not turn up, what do you do? Your department will have in place a set of procedures for you – or someone else – to follow. You need to find out what these are in advance. You will have to tell students what they are, what the consequences of missing tutorials will be, if any, and how they can make up for missed sessions, if that applies in your course.

Listening and responding, observing, questioning, paraphrasing, summarising, standing back, biting your tongue, letting students make mistakes, prompting, timekeeping, defining, giving instructions, encouraging, praising, establishing and maintaining ground rules, refocusing, chairing, correcting: you may be doing all these things, and more, during a one-hour tutorial, even if you delegate some of these functions to students.

   Listening and responding is obviously about hearing and replying to what students say. Ideas do not necessarily emerge in a logical stream, so keeping notes during discussion, possibly with a seating diagram, can help you attribute ideas to individuals when giving feedback. However, do not underestimate the importance of non-verbal cues which you can use to encourage interaction and contributions:

- looking around the group;
- nodding;
- smiling;
- hand signals.

You can use signals to prompt students to speak or to block students who are about to interrupt, using eye contact – and removal of eye contact – to avoid becoming the 'filter' of student comments. When one student speaks, initially the others may look directly at you, to see what your judgement is. When this happens, you may redirect their attention to each other.

When the students are doing something, then you can be doing and saying nothing. Staying in the background, or apparently getting on with another task, so that you don't look like you are eavesdropping, is another non-verbal strategy for prompting students to get on with the task.

Using questions is an excellent way to stimulate students to think and can 'oil' the processes of group discussion. Developing skills of good questioning probably will require practice, and the type of question you ask should be carefully chosen to fit your intentions. If, for example, you are trying to draw out students' contributions, you may wish to ask an elaborating or clarifying question.

Closed questions usually offer little scope for response ('When did Henry VIII of England die?') Be aware that if you ask a closed question, it may partly explain why students do not respond, or only respond in minimal terms. For example, if you ask 'Did you read the assignment?', then the answer is either yes or no. No further discussion need follow. Open questions, such as the examples of elaborating questions (below), allow more scope for response. You can, of course, practise different types of question to see how students respond, using, for example, the options shown below.

Questioning strategies for group learning

Testing

To check the following:

- knowledge: Which critics have described X as a comedy?
- comprehension: What do you think this author means by …?

- application: How might this theory be used in …?
- analysis: What functions do they have in common?
- synthesis: Could you summarise what we have said so far?
- evaluation: Which of these do you feel is best and why?

Elaborating

Encouraging students to explain more:

- Can you tell me more about that?
- What does that make you feel?

Clarifying

To ensure a shared understanding:

- What did you mean by …?
- Can you give me an example?

Reasoning

To justify or provide a rationale:

- Why did you choose this approach?

Comparative

To focus on similarities and differences:

- How would your results compare with the published ones?

Opinion-seeking

To stimulate debate.

- What is your view on …?

Over time, you will probably develop your own repertoire of 'questions that work'. Brookfield and Preskill (1999) offer good advice about honing your skills of questioning, listening and responding. No doubt, you will even more quickly form insights into forms of questioning that, in some sense or another, do not work. These are the ones that stifle rather than encourage student discussion. Again, you may find that you have your own collection of errors that you – and perhaps tutors you have known – have made, but this list may help you to avoid them altogether.

Common errors in questioning

- Asking too many questions at once.
- Asking a question and answering it yourself.
- Asking questions only of the brightest or most likeable.
- Asking a difficult question too early.
- Asking irrelevant questions.
- Always asking the same types of questions.
- Not indicating a change in the type of question.
- Not using probing questions.
- Not giving time to think.
- Not correcting wrong answers.
- Ignoring answers.
- Failing to see the implications of answers.
- Failing to build on answers.

(Brown and Atkins, 1988)

Finally, make sure that you leave time for reinforcing the learning: sum up, relate the discussion to the learning outcomes, give praise, or prompt your students to probe their own learning by summarising and rechecking that the aims and outcomes of the session have been met, identifying follow-up tasks for yourself and for students. A transitional question for you to ask, as you move the discussion into this final phase, could be 'Where are we going from here?'

What problems do postgraduate tutors worry about?

I was unused to dealing with groups and my anxiety focused on my own performance.

In workshops and discussions students raise many different problems. Some of these appear to result from lack of information or experience; others may be the understandable result of anxiety about their first teaching task. Following are examples of typical problems.

Problems

- The whole group is silent and unresponsive.
- Individuals are silent and unresponsive.
- The group expects the tutor to do it all.
- Students have not done the preparation or don't know what they should have done.
- Students do not answer when you ask a question.
- One or more students are very dominant and hog the discussion.
- The group picks on one student in an aggressive way.
- Discussion goes off the point and becomes irrelevant.
- Students don't see the relevance of the discussion.
- Students don't take you seriously.
- Students reject the discussion process and demand answers.
- Discussion focuses on one part of the group and the rest stop joining in.
- Subgroups start forming private conversations.
- Group members do not listen to each other.
- The discussion does not build on previous contributions.
- Students complain about the tutorial and the way you are handling it.
- Students are visibly bored.

It is not our intention to provide solutions to all these problems. There are other resources where you can find useful suggestions (Jacques, 2000; Tiberius, 1999). However, many of the difficulties with student behaviours, such as aggression or dominance, can be dealt with by setting appropriate ground rules at the beginning. One of the ground rules could be that students will listen to what others have to say, so that as soon as they begin to interrupt each other you can refer back to the ground rules that you all agreed to at the beginning.

This may not always work. One solution will not solve all the problems. Another way you can deal with dominance is to ask the quieter members of the group to make a contribution first. If the same students continue to dominate, you will have to speak to them individually, explaining that they are not allowing others in the group to speak.

Silence and unresponsiveness can usually be dealt with by initially putting students into pairs as the first step in any task, so that they move to the next stage of the group work with a shared contribution, which makes them both feel safer. That usually deals with the situation where either the whole group or individuals are silent.

What can you do when students do not read or prepare for the discussion? Be realistic about what you are asking students to do out of class. They may simply have too much to do. Check that they are clear about how to do the task. Even 'reading' tasks can be confusing, if students are not sure about what they are supposed to do: summarise, evaluate, compare and contrast with other readings? If they simply have not done it, let them read a bit of it there and then. Get them writing about what they have read for five minutes; make that private writing, for their own use only, but as a trigger for discussions. You can also set them a straightforward – or complex – question to write about. Setting a distinct task that they can do in five minutes is a good way of getting them to engage with the material. Or you could ask them to summarise in five minutes the main points of a previous lecture. Above all, avoid taking over and filling in for them.

This means that you have to prepare not only the task for the tutorial, but also one or more alternative activities. Once you have done that, you will be able to deal with the problem of lack of preparation, you will be less anxious if the students are not ready to participate, and you will be able to help them achieve some of the learning outcomes. As time goes by, you will develop a repertoire of such alternatives and be better able to match them to the specific objectives of the course. Remember also that 'summarise' is a deceptively simple instruction: watch how your students manage it.

'What can I do if the students don't take me seriously?' This is something that worries postgraduates, particularly those who look young. The giggling, the cynical smile and other non-verbals are designed, it seems, to signal to you that your students are not interested in what you are saying. This may be one of a number of more personal questions, about your credibility or your sense of your perceived credibility. The students will take you seriously if they see that you are well prepared and organised and have a knowledge of the literature base. Having said that, you may feel that you are having to ignore their reactions, focusing on the work to be done, and perhaps even that you are still earning credibility. This may be a goal of the first couple of tutorials; rather than waiting years till you acquire credibility, if you show your students right from the start that you are taking a professional approach, you may earn their trust quite quickly. Above all, try not to get into the habit of apologising. It is a trait observed among postgraduates, and by postgraduates, that they tend to apologise more than they need to. This is not to say that you should never apologise, but you should not make it a kind of verbal habit.

What do you do about a culture clash, with increasingly international groups of students in the same class? This can, of course, make for very interesting discussions, but there may be clashes of values. There may be issues here that you are not equipped to deal with. Ground rules are again the key. Talk to others in the department: this will be an issue not just in your class but in other classes too, and this is an area where a unified and informed approach is key.

There may be problems you have contributed to yourself. Perhaps you talked too much at an early session and have, without meaning to, taken over. This does not, of course, make you the 'control freak' tutor, but it might have had a shaping effect on your students' behaviours. This may be why they appear at your next tutorial expecting you to do all the talking. One solution is explicitly to shift your role: 'Last week I told you about ... I gave you background for today's task of ...'. For this to work well, you may have to give your students time to recap on what you said last time. They can do this in small groups. You may have to let them proceed with partial summaries of what you said. If your aim is to get them working on a group task, get them on to that as quickly as possible.

There may, of course, be problems that you cannot solve. You may need to ask for help or support. For example, if a student behaves in an aggressive manner towards you, or towards other students, and has not acted on your suggestions for changing their behaviour – that is, your first step has to be asking them to change – you may feel ill-equipped to deal with the situation. You may feel unsafe, in which case, say so. You can draw a line. Say, 'Your behaviour is not appropriate ... I feel threatened by what you said ... by how you talked to me when you said ...'.

Accept the fact that you are not going to be able to deal with every single problem that you are presented with. Remember that you have rights – you may choose to make a formal complaint about a student – but this is an extreme we all try to avoid. You are not expected to be some 'super-tutor', particularly in your first semester of teaching. Do not expect too much of yourself. Once you are clear about where the limit of acceptable behaviour lies, and once you have communicated that to students, you might find that some of the problems resolve themselves. You will have more self-assurance, knowing what types of student behaviour you do not need to tolerate, and you will probably convey more confidence to your students as a result.

Nor can you solve all your students' problems. They may have personal problems that disrupt their learning in groups. Do not get out of your depth. Find out what support services there are. Direct your students to those services. Do not feel that you have to be their counsellor. These issues are covered in more detail in Chapter 7.

Evaluating learning and teaching in tutorials

The techniques are not going to be very different from evaluating your lectures, except that in tutorials you have an opportunity for the group to evaluate together. You can evaluate learning by using the techniques we described at the end of Chapter 2, and Jacques (2000) includes a number of suggestions. These will work well in tutorials, and you need to know what strategies are helping your students to learn.

The focus also is on evaluating your skills, on your role as a group facilitator. That is what you need feedback on at this stage. Because it is a complex situation, you could focus on one aspect of the event, such as 'Did I choose an appropriate activity for the learning outcomes?'

Self-evaluation checklist

- Did I ask questions which stimulated lively discussion?
- Did I manage the time well?
- Did students all participate in discussion and tasks?
- Were there any difficulties?
- What would I change if I were to do this again?
- What notes do I want to make for the next time around?

How do you develop your own self-evaluation checklist? Do you create a mix of (1) questions about what you did and (2) what you observed students doing, or do you (3) focus on one or the other? You can use variations on the self-evaluation checklist to get feedback from your students by asking specific questions. Ask your students to write for a couple of minutes on each question.

Student evaluation questions

- Did you enjoy that activity/task?
- Which aspects of the group activity worked well?

- Which aspects did not work well?
- What skills do you think you are developing as a result of the group work?
- What is the most important thing you learned today?

You may find that your department issues a final, end-of-semester questionnaire to students. However, you are probably – you can check – at liberty to conduct a bit of evaluation before the end of your first semester of tutorial teaching, for obvious reasons.

There are lots of pro formas available, but sometimes the simplest are the best. You can always make up your own questions. If you want to be really focused, perhaps asking students to answer one question is enough. That would also take up less class time.

Portfolio

What do you do with the results? What can you learn from student feedback? How do you go about this business of 'reflection'? It is not enough simply to describe your teaching goals and performance, or to assert that your teaching has resulted in your students learning.

While the activities of student evaluation and self-evaluation are important for your professional development and conduct, you need to begin to think about what constitutes evidence of good teaching:

- How do you know what your students are learning?
- How does their learning relate to your teaching?
- How do you know that your teaching is improving?
- How do you convince others that it is?

This is not just about persuading others that you are a great teacher; it is about demonstrating that you are effective in this role. It is also about having evidence – and confidence – that your teaching is reaching an appropriate standard. There is personal value in having evidence so that you know what you are achieving.

We should flag up here that this is a step change from the descriptive elements of your portfolio suggested in the previous two chapters. In order genuinely to evaluate your teaching, you need evidence and criteria for performance. Where will you find these criteria: in the discipline/department handbook, among your personal goals or external benchmarks, from professional organisations (try their websites)? Once you have the criteria, the question is what constitutes evidence.

There are, of course, many types of evidence of good teaching, or of developing teaching skills, since becoming a 'good teacher' is not necessarily a goal that has a distinct endpoint. There is always room for improvement. Each new student cohort presents new challenges. When you start a new semester, no matter how much teaching experience you have had, you are, in a sense, starting from scratch.

Once you have collected some student feedback, you have to devise some way of analysing it. For example, when you look at your students' responses to the one-minute paper (see Chapters 2 and 10), you might record and reflect on:

- how many responses you got;
- what main themes arise from them;
- how these themes relate to your and the course's intended learning outcomes;
- how you will respond to this feedback – what one action you will take.

For your portfolio, describe the relationship between what you did in your tutorials and the literature, any reading you did about tutorials – even your reading of this chapter – and your understanding of the characteristics of good practice in tutorials. The following quotation is an example of the type of thing you could write for your portfolio:

Relate your use of a particular practice to the literature

Throughout the session I tried to give time for the students to present their ideas, and to absorb the points made both by myself and by other group members. Leaving pauses and being tolerant of silences is highlighted by Brockbank and McGill (1998) as a key skill to be achieved by a facilitator of group work.

You may be able to make a case not only for the activities and strategies you used, but also against those that you decided not to use, giving your rationale:

Give your rationale for rejecting alternative approaches on this occasion

A didactic approach to teaching this session would undermine effective learning and inevitably stifle the students who have done more courses in this area and want to move on quickly. I wanted to use group work because it would encourage participation, reduce physical distance, bring the class together socially and let them move through the material at different rates.

Or you could write about lessons you learned along the way, and where you see, looking back, that you could have done better:

Identify areas where you could improve

Jacques (2000) asserts the importance of structuring group work to encourage shy, difficult or less dominant members of the group to participate. A particularly forthcoming student from the first group volunteered without hesitation to comment on their work, and would have gone on to dominate her group's contribution had I not intervened to try and encourage more even participation. The students in the second group were far less eager to volunteer to speak, which I now realise could have been avoided if we had decided at the start who would speak.

Finally, if you have just started teaching, there are bound to be questions about teaching and learning that you cannot yet answer. Identify these. Consider what you might do to find out more. In practice, your experience of teaching may have thrown up new questions. Again, record these and develop strategies for working out solutions. Prioritise the ones you must work on in the short term and identify those that can wait.

Identify areas for your future study and development

Working alongside many different lecturers delivering this programme, I am aware that my approach is not consistent. I have found myself struggling either to get a word in – as the tutor I should have control of the floor – or to 'think on my feet' – as I suddenly clam up and 20 curious students are waiting in anticipation for my pearls of wisdom. However, that discussion is for another day.

Such ongoing questioning will not, of course, stop once you have more teaching experience. Instead, you will continue to ask questions about what worked, what failed and why, throughout your career. This is not a sign of lack of confidence, but a characteristic of an inquiring approach and a professional attitude towards teaching.

Additional resources

Brookfield, S. and Preskill, S. (1999) *Discussion as a Way of Teaching: Tools and Techniques for University Teachers*. Buckingham: SRHE and Open University Press.
An intelligent, in-depth discussion of discussion.

Jacques, D. (2000) *Learning in Groups*, 3rd edn. London: Kogan Page.
An excellent resource for everyone who is managing learning in groups, with both theory and practical suggestions for success. One for your bookshelf.

4

Your First Electronic Discussions

Students are more comfortable with the face-to-face interaction they had at school, even if in reality this is a luxury in many universities. (O'Leary, 2004: 3)

The trend to 'online anything' is powerful and difficult to resist. (Stephenson, 2001: x)

Both of these quotes express the tensions and excitement associated with the rapid growth in electronic learning or e-learning. As a researcher and learner you may be only too familiar with this dichotomy. You will probably hear academic colleagues expressing a range of views – some, like O'Leary's, quite contentious – about the role of e-learning in universities:

- Will it replace face-to-face teaching?
- Will there come a day when it relieves staff from teaching and makes time for research?
- Is this simply another resource for learning and teaching, doing the same thing, but faster and on a larger scale?
- How do we know if it really improves student learning?

E-learning is, for many academics, a controversial subject, and you may find that the debate has become polarised: some will argue that e-learning removes direct personal contact with, and among, students; conversely, others will say that it increases student–tutor interaction. Nor is this simply a theoretical debate, since there is concern that e-learning, far from saving time and money, currently consumes more of both than traditional teaching methods do.

To complicate matters further, undergraduate student numbers have increased – in some institutions, dramatically. At the same time, there seems to be a trend towards reducing weekly tutorials or labs. In these circumstances, e-learning may be helpful: it can enable direct access to tutors and electronic discussion with their peers.

Another recent trend, widening access to higher education, brings new demands for additional support for disabled students and students from non-traditional backgrounds: forms of e-learning may help us to provide that support. For students on distance-learning courses, electronic discussions can create the group work that they would otherwise miss out on. Moreover, for students with caring responsibilities or part-time jobs, technology provides a means of accessing tutors and colleagues 'beyond office hours' (Nomdo, 2004: 208).

This sketch of current contextual issues is intended to help you steer your way through such debates, although you may be wondering whether it might be more sensible for you to plot a course away from them altogether. Yet you should have some form of 'critical engagement' with the technology currently used in university teaching (Nomdo, 2004: 205), especially if you are intending to progress an academic career.

E-learning is one of the fastest changing and most unpredictable areas in learning and teaching, and we do not yet fully understand the impact that new technology will have. This can, therefore, be one of the most exciting areas you are involved in, with real opportunities to be creative and innovative. You may find that you get caught up in the potential of new technology. In other words, while there might be a risk of overinvesting in this teaching role – in terms of time and energy – you might really enjoy it and make a name for yourself as an enthusiast or 'expert'.

In writing this chapter, we assume that your role is most likely to be that of e-tutor or e-moderator. That is, you are the person who facilitates electronic activities and discussion, rather than the one who designs and administers the course. The topics we cover are intended to give you an introduction to the context of that role, the nature of your responsibilities, practical information about getting started, advice for your portfolio and sources of more information. Within the scope of this book, we can do little more than help you on your way and point you to further resources.

Some key aspects of effective e-learning environments

It has been argued that e-learning is learning from experience using a new medium with access to a range of new resources (Alexander and Boud, 2001). If you accept this – and we do – many of the principles of good practice which apply to face-to-face learning and teaching also apply in the electronic environment. Key features of e-learning should include opportunities for active engagement, peer discussion and collaboration, intellectual challenges and a learning environment which values each participant. Apart from the huge number of resources available, particular advantages of e-learning are that it is time and place independent, may place people on an equal footing, allows time for reflection and considered responses to discussion, and permits the process of learning to become more visible because all dialogue is conserved. Thus students are enabled to construct their own learning through reflection and interaction with their peers using a range of activities but in a different way; this may suit some students' learning styles better than face-to-face situations.

What is different is the fact that individuals are communicating in an environment where they are unlikely to see faces or hear voices, and they are doing this through technology, which may in itself present barriers. What is more, they may be off-campus, with little or no local support, and they may be online at any time, day or night. For these main reasons, and others, effective electronic learning environments rely on great attention paid to:

- An appropriate fit with the context. The advantages of using the electronic medium must be evident to both students and staff, otherwise they will not use it. This is done by exploiting the special features the technology offers and minimising the limitations.
- Course design which: has clear aims and outcomes; is well structured, user friendly and attractively presented; includes a variety of activities; develops a learning community through online group discussion; gives guidance and support; gives feedback on progress; and integrates assessment.
- Extended resources, such as online access to library holdings, the internet, electronic databases, etc.
- Tutors who have appropriate knowledge and skills to facilitate online learning.

(McAlpine et al., 2004; Mason, 2001)

It is probable that you will have no influence or responsibility for the context, course design and resources available to students in your department; therefore you can concentrate on your role as e-tutor.

What does e-learning mean in your department at this time?

E-learning has taken an unexpected turn. It has not, as promised, replaced campus-based learning, but it has pioneered a 'pick-and-mix' approach to teaching and studying. (Weller, 2004: 4)

As this quote implies, the implementation of e-learnng is taking many forms, from courses that are fully online to those that are 'blended' with face-to-face classes. This may be the case in your department, where staff are exploring the potential of the technology. You may find any or all of these types of e-resources:

- lecture notes on the web;
- PowerPoint slides on the web;
- recorded lecturer in webcasts – for revision or catch-up;
- simulations to consolidate learning;
- revision activities;
- problems, case studies, scenarios;
- student group projects, discussions or chat;
- student peer review;
- interactive classrooms;
- virtual classrooms or other virtual environments.

Which of these are offered in your department? You will probably not be asked to develop new e-learning materials, but you might want to know who has produced materials and to discuss with them how they see those resources being used: what worked, where are the glitches, who fixes them? Colleagues in e-learning may be your most important resource. Even those who are just starting out, like yourself, can share strategies and solutions.

Is there evidence in your department that e-learning changed student behaviour or that it identified new needs? Have lecturers in your department modified teaching approaches accordingly? Is there an e-learning strategy in action in your department? Is everyone committed to this? Or is your e-tutoring an isolated – or experimental – example?

Your department – and/or institution – should have an e-learning strategy. How that is being implemented, and how it is resourced, particularly in terms of technical support, are key questions which may be beyond your remit at this stage, but your colleagues' answers may help you understand exactly what is meant by e-learning in your department.

Your role in e-tutoring

As an e-tutor, or e-moderator, you may be managing student discussion of, for example, a topic set by the lecturer teaching the course. Your first step is to establish what your role involves:

- providing information;
- (setting and) managing structured work, such as problem-solving;
- prompting discussion and/or tasks;
- moderating a student discussion;
- encouraging and motivating;
- negotiating;
- taking the role of different characters;
- advising;
- managing a virtual community or simulated environment.

You may find that you are expected to manage more than one, if not all, of these tasks, since they may all be a part of online group activities. Perhaps, on the surface, they do not look very different from tasks required to manage face-to-face tutorials (Chapter 3). However, because you won't be able to use facial expressions, body language, speech and observation as tools to enable understanding, you will have to rely only on the written word. Careful attention to detail matters.

Just as you would expect if you were facilitating face-to-face tutorials, you should expect to be briefed about the course or module (see Chapter 3) and the online elements. Your department will provide guidelines on your role, and these should give you general information about how e-facilitation differs from face-to-face tutorials or labs in your discipline. An excellent resource for those managing e-discussions can be found at the JISC InfoNet website (http://www.jiscinfonet.ac.uk/InfoKits/effective-use-of-VLEs). Ideally, you will also be told the focus for discussions, with perhaps links to lectures or other parts of the course and materials to use for prompting discussion. If you have seen none of this, then ask the module coordinator.

Questions to ask the module coordinator

- What is the purpose and focus of the e-discussion?
- How does it relate to the rest of the course?
- Are the students set tasks to prepare for the discussions?
- Have they been briefed about their roles and tasks?
- Are there other e-discussions to give me an idea of what happens?
- How do e-discussions relate to courseworks and assessments?
- How often and for how long am I required to participate?
- Do I have time to get used to the environment before the sessions start?

- Is all the material I will need available online?
- Will I have to do any research for this tutoring?
- Will there be formal training or a 'walk through' the material?
- Will that include hands-on experience of the environment?
- Is there an archive (of discussions) I can access?
- Whom do I contact if I or my students have problems?
- Are there likely to be any disabled students on this module?
- If so, what resources are there to support disabled students?

With luck, someone in the department may have previous experience of assisting e-learning and could act as your mentor. You may also find information through an online tutors' discussion forum. This is where you can discuss more detailed questions about matters like 'tone'. What tone should you use in your interventions? How exactly can you strike that tone? What specific words should you use? Are there things that do not work: are there tutor contributions that failed to stimulate student discussion, for example? Or how have other tutors guided students to learn from their mistakes? You can start to answer these question by using strategies covered in the previous chapter on group learning, but there will be specific implementations that have worked or failed in the e-learning environment your department uses. Find out what they are.

Do you have the skills for e-tutoring?

Many of the skills you need for e-tutoring are those you would be expected to have for face-to-face tutoring, albeit in an online environment (Salmon, 2004):

- content knowledge, so that you can direct students to relevant resources (the web or multimedia), steer the discussion and keep it focused, generate pertinent questions and interject current or emerging information;
- communication skills, such as courtesy, politeness and respect, valuing diversity and ability to write clearly and concisely;
- personal characteristics such as enthusiasm, confidence and sensitivity to relationships;
- understanding of discussion processes which require developing and enabling others, building online trust, summarising, restating, challenging, exploring ideas, managing threading, controlling and letting go, pacing discussion.

What is different, of course, is that you will need technical skills, including good keyboard skills, and the ability to navigate around online structures of the web and electronic learning environments and to link the discussion with other online features. Do you know how to set up topic areas within the discussion space? Do you know how to thread messages? Do you know how to close off and archive discussions? Do you know how to deal with attachments?

Many postgraduates have a high level of word processing and other IT skills. However, different formats, software or structures can create problems and take up a huge amount of your time. Ask for formal and/or informal help:

1 Get on a course.
2 Find a mentor/buddy.
3 Ask for a demonstration.
4 Observe others.
5 Negotiate your role.

As you become familiar with the system, you will quickly become aware that it is equally important that you have the right equipment. Do you have the necessary hardware and software to be an e-tutor on this course? Are they fast enough, for example? If not, ask for a loan – or an upgrade – from your department. Make the case that you cannot afford time to sort out glitches or find ways around technical problems.

Interactive e-learning: getting started

As for any other form of teaching, you will have been given some guidance on the aim or purpose of interactive e-learning. If not, ask whether its purpose is for students to:

- familiarise themselves with the online environment;
- share knowledge;
- answer questions;
- discuss a topic;
- work collaboratively;
- learn from their mistakes;
- evaluate their knowledge.

You may find that it is all of these, and if this is the case, we suggest you talk to your module coordinator or course leader to make sure you are well briefed about what is expected and what resources are already available. We discussed planning

TABLE 4.1

The five-step model of learning and teaching through computer mediated conferencing (Salmon, 2002; 2004)

STEP	STUDENTS	E-MODERATOR
1 Access and motivation	Gain access and participate	Welcomes and encourages
2 Socialisation	Establish online identity and contact others	Familiarises and bridges cultural, social and learning environments
3 Information exchange	Search, personalise software, exchange course-related information	Facilitates tasks and supports use of learning resources
4 Knowledge construction	Engage in group discussion and collaborative interaction	Facilitates processes; builds and sustains groups
5 Development	Integrate discussion with other forms of learning; construct learning; reflect; achieve personal goals	Responds and provides support

for group work in the previous chapter, which will give you a start with planning; however, you will need to think thoroughly and in detail about what you and your students will do online.

Based on her extensive research of managing discussion groups, Gilly Salmon (2002; 2004) has proposed a straightforward five-step model of learning and teaching through computer mediated conferencing (CMC) (Table 4.1). You can use this model to help you think about your e-tutoring tasks. As with any other form of teaching, advance planning and preparation are just as important as 'doing'. There are other more complex models for e-tutoring (Laurillard, 2002; Mayes and Fowler, 1999) which you may wish to explore.

Enabling access and motivating students

Your role at this stage is to help your students access the discussion space and stimulate them to get involved. Be enthusiastic and welcoming. Your students will differ in their IT skills, knowledge of your department's systems and confidence. Therefore, it will be important for you to provide information about how to get online and to motivate and encourage students to 'dive in'. You will also have to ensure your students get the technical help they need. If your students attend class on campus, you can use the first class to support them through this stage. If not, you can use email or the telephone. Importantly, if you have any disabled students on your module, attend to their needs; if you do not know exactly what to do, seek help.

Outline of your first discussion with students

- How to log in.
- How the environment is structured.
- What spaces are available to them to use.
  - 'Here are the social conversation spaces.'
  - 'Here's where you do your academic work.'
- 'Here's the handbook to help you if you forget.'
- 'Here's what to do/whom to contact if it does not work.'

The thing that seems to worry postgraduate e-tutors most, quite rightly, is what to do when things go wrong, especially at the beginning. If a student phones up and says they cannot log on, how will you deal with that? Is there a WebCT administrator, for example? You must have a name, a telephone number and an email address to pass to your students so that they can request technical assistance, otherwise they will quickly get frustrated.

One difference with e-learning, which influences how people use it, is the expectation of an instant response and an instant fix. While many of us are only too aware of technology's capacity to break down, there is still the expectation that it should work, and quickly – that it should, at least, make things more efficient. Consequently, when things do go wrong, users are not patient. They will quickly reject a system that has regular glitches. In other words, even when you and your students have the necessary skills and equipment, there may still be problems. Fixing these will be beyond your remit. Your students need to know that they should not contact you with technical problems – they would simply be wasting their time (and yours).

Try to remember that social skills may go into the background, as keyboard and navigation skills come to the foreground. Some students will get through this stage quickly, others will take more time. You may have to reassure them if they are anxious about the technology (McConnell, 2005). For that to work, it is important that you are not only visibly checking their participation but also responding to it. Your role in providing feedback and motivation is as important in this medium as in any other. How you describe and analyse this interaction is worth considering for your teaching portfolio.

Socialising

Once all your students are online and communicating with you, you can move on. At this point your goal is to build an electronic community where all students will feel comfortable. This will take time as they get accustomed to a new surrounding and new people and their own identity in what, for some, will be a rather alien environment where there are no verbal or visual cues; they will need to 'find their place' and establish relationships.

Initial briefing for students: what to tell them

Is participation compulsory or voluntary?

- Will participation be assessed?
- If so, what are the assessment criteria?
- Do they have the option of opting out of e-learning?

How do students participate?

- How long will discussions last?
- What is the structure of the whole activity?
- What is expected of them during the whole duration?
- Can they write informally?
- Can they use abbreviations?
- Do they have to use correct grammar, spell check etc.?
- How will e-learning benefit them?

How will you, the tutor, participate?

- Will you answer their questions or comment on their participation?
- What kind of cues will you give them (since visual ones are not possible)?

If at all possible, use a face-to-face session for this stage:

- Get all your students together for a meeting, so that they start getting to know each other as they go online together. Use this opportunity to discuss the questions given in the box so that expectations are clarified.
- Let them get involved in social discussions. Give them a topic to talk about. Introduce them to the online resources. They should find this helpful because they will probably all confront the same issues when they start using the system.
- Introduce them all to the technical aspects of the system for accessing, sending and receiving information.
- Discuss the rules of behaviour, or 'netiquette'.

As for other forms of group work, ground rules can help students understand their responsibilities. In e-discussion it is particularly important to exercise respect and courtesy, value everyone's contributions, and use appropriate language and tone.

Make the netiquette clear to them by explaining that their communications should be more like a letter than spontaneous speech (or whatever you think it is). This means that when they interact with each other they need to construct their conversations with some thought. It is not just free-flow: 'The person at the other end has no non-verbal communication. All they have is your words.' Can you run through examples of what this all means for them in practice? Can you get examples from colleagues in your department? Illustrating what is – and is not – acceptable will have more impact than simply describing it.

If a student does express strong feelings, or uses improper or offensive language (sometimes called 'flaming'), deal with it immediately through email; do not use the shared discussion space to reprimand individuals. However, it may be appropriate, if not necessary, to ask for a 'public' apology from the offender.

When you feel you are ready to move your students onto the next stage and get them started on course-related activities, remind them that they have an informal 'chat' or 'café' space for their social conversations and to allocate tasks, share notes of work done for group projects, set up meetings and so on. Academic work will be done in the main discussion area.

Exchanging course-related information

Students should now be ready to engage with the course content and their peers, and they can be working entirely online. You will be directing them to all the resources that support their study, and encouraging them to explore and share their knowledge. However, structure will be necessary to prevent them from getting lost or distracted.

Setting the first e-discussion task for your students

1 Set your students a straightforward task at the start – a question or topic for discussion, for example. Salmon (2004: 31) suggests that the task might be about 'discovering or exploring known (to them) answers, or … aspects of problems or issues'. See also Salmon (2002) and Buckner and Morss (1999).

2 Make your instructions for the task crystal clear, since they may not have an immediate opportunity to clarify what you mean. They must know exactly what they have to do; if they try to post something at midnight, they will not be able to ask you for clarification. While this is obvious, get your students to think about the implications for their work patterns.

3 Give them, or have them design, timelines for the task. Help them to define stages. Get them to treat this like a face-to-face class in that respect. It is not enough to tell them that 'time management is important in e-learning'; make sure that they find ways to set milestones. For this and future tasks you might decide to set/suggest some for them.

4 Once the discussion is under way, go in and be part of it. Show that you are there. Designate set times and days when you will do this, so that students know that you can answer questions then. It is important to have a regular slot, so they know that they have not just been left to get on with it on their own. This will also help you to plan and manage your work.

Your students will expect you to give direction and encouragement as they begin to explore the potential of the medium, and you may get floods of messages. They may be demanding help searching and selecting or sending questions about where to find things. You will need to impose some discipline, in spite of possible instincts to provide immediate assistance, otherwise you may never get offline.

Tutors need to develop their facilitation skills to be successful online. Ways of limiting the demands on their time need to be sought, otherwise 'interaction fatigue' leads to early burnout. (Mason, 2001: 75)

Even in the discussion, you do not have to be constantly checking or available. Because discussions are threaded you can catch up after a break of a day or two. This lets you get on with your own work. Explain this to students, so that they do not build up false expectations. If they want you to be more available, you will have to hold your ground, and you may benefit from the support of someone else in your department at that point.

First tasks like this also can reveal a range of problems, skills gaps and glitches, many of which you will help with, but some you may not be able to fix. As you are the students' first point of contact, it will be you they ask. Be ready to pass their queries on to someone who can help, especially if there are technical problems.

Electronic discussion is good for immediate follow-up to lectures and presentations. It is a format that students are likely to be familiar with. Associations of informality may help to motivate students to participate, and you can point out any turning points in the discussion, interesting ways of personalising knowledge, or important differences of view or bodies of evidence. Although it might be tempting to use the informality of chat space for these discussions, it has been argued that chat is less useful for in-depth consideration of a topic (Clarke, 2004), and students may get confused.

These discussions may be opportunities for your students to create new knowledge – that is, 'new' to them – as they make new connections, for example. If you are not sure how their wide-ranging comments and probing questions relate to the prescribed topic of the discussion, then it may be good enough for you to say just that and to prompt them to make links and draw boundaries between points. As in other forms of teaching, it is not up to you to be the world expert on either the discussion topic or the medium of learning; what is important is that you prompt students to make connections and draw distinctions. This includes prompting them to make connections with what they have studied in other courses or modules. They also have to have, at some stage, a basis for their answers, and establishing that can become almost a routine prompt from you or, you may find, from each other.

Knowledge construction and development

By now, your students should be interacting with each other, actively engaging in learning by posting ideas, accepting criticism, debating, expanding thoughts, reshaping concepts, integrating and synthesising content. Now you can really develop your facilitation skills to sustain and nurture the group, as you weave the contributions to provide direction, provoke further debate through questioning, and summarise. You interject new topics and stimulate new thoughts, introduce new themes. But you must also be mindful to close discussion when they have run their course.

Questioning and responding to students

See Chapter 3 for:

- Ways of asking good questions – questions that work well to prompt student discussion – and responding to the answers. Then, whether or not the students act on your prompts is something you will be able to observe: 'The best source of information on the pedagogical value of the learning materials used will come from the way students carry out assignments based on them' (Laurillard, 2002: 237).
- Ways of responding to students' comments. For example, where a student has clearly done some follow-up work or thinking, in response to your remarks, what general or specific positive comments would you make? What would you say – if anything – if students have clearly not done a follow-up task?

As your students become more and more confident, they will take on greater responsibility for their learning. They may request faster services or more software and become more demanding of the system. They may relax and you may see more affective elements of their discussion. It may become more obvious to you that students are constructing their own learning (see Chapter 1) by making connections with other knowledge bases. They may also feel comfortable to openly discuss complex issues of a social and ethical nature. You can keep them moving forward by promoting critical thinking and setting challenging tasks.

More on managing electronic discussions

A critical factor ... is that you cannot see the other participants. This removes the richness of non-verbal communication (e.g. knowing when the other person wants to speak, disagrees with your comments or is simply not interested). (Clarke, 2004: 193)

This is a point we have mentioned before. While it may be true, as Clarke argues, that you can lose the 'richness' of face-to-face contact that you get in tutorials and labs, for example, e-learning can also remove students' inhibitions. Some will be more willing to write what they think in an e-discussion group, a format that many will find more familiar, than they would be to talk in a tutorial. For others, the opposite may be true: they do not want to put their thoughts in writing to a peer group.

Once discussion is under way, what types of interventions will you make? Ask more experienced colleagues what they do and how students respond when they do that. Will you correct errors or not? Will you comment on digressions or not? Will you let your students find these for themselves? Is that part of the task? Will you make that specific for them? Are you able to outline the different types of learning they can do in different ways? Do you tell them, in advance, that multiple framings of questions, different solutions to problems, and paradoxes and tensions are part of this mode of learning? Or do you let them find ways to deal with all this for themselves?

What kind of 'safety net' will you provide, if any? Can you map out for them what their e-learning process will look like? Will you use e-learning for revision or not? Above all, do not set about answering all the students' questions on your own, unless you have had training and/or have been advised to do so by your department. Seek advice. Learn from others. Do not reinvent the wheel.

Questions for the e-tutor

- Will you allow different frames of reference, different terms and versions of concepts to run for a time in discussions?
- How will you bring your students back to the focal point, without dampening their enthusiasm?
- How will you ensure that they progress with the learning outcomes of the course or module?

Overall, therefore, it may be a matter not of losing the 'richness' of face-to-face communication but of finding other 'richnesses' or, perhaps more importantly, helping the students to find and exploit them. Perhaps equally important, however, is the question of whether or not your students see e-learning as different from other types of learning. Do they see the intended integration of e-learning and other activities? Is that something that you will have to prompt them to discuss and/or work out? Can you ask them, not just because you do not know, but in order to check what they know? Can you find out if they need any special support without providing all that support yourself?

Integrating web-based resources into your e-discussions

Not all e-learning is interactive. There are millions of web-based resources out there, as you will know. In addition, your department might have web-based resources for courses on which you tutor. To complicate, or enrich, matters further, your students will find and use websites you have never heard of. In this fascinatingly complex context, the best thing you can do is to make the learning more interactive by including the use of these resources in your e-tutoring discussions. It may not be enough simply to tell students that a specific resource exists. Even recommending one, or telling them that it is related to a specific part of the course, will not ensure that they use it. Effective use of a web-based resource involves integrating it in the course. For example, students can prepare presentations and dissertations using three websites:

- slide presentations: http://www.strath.ac.uk/Departments/CAP/ slides/intro.html;
- poster presentations: http://www.strath.ac.uk/Departments/CAP/ poster/intro.html;
- dissertation writing: http://www.strath.ac.uk/Departments/CAP/ dissertation/intro.html.

Each of these sites – or others like them – has proved effective in helping students complete coursework and presentations. However, if you simply tell them where the sites are, it is unlikely that they will do more than take a look at them, if that. If, on the other hand, you ask them to set milestones in their preparation, in the form of interim deadlines, and if you monitor their performance at these deadlines, or if they report on their progress with stages in the task at these milestones, they are more likely to use them. In this way, you help students to develop the skills they need.

The steps you can take are as follows:

- Talk the students through the structure of the website you want them to use or think might help them with their tasks. The websites listed above have flowcharts you can use to do this. Tell them where everything is, how they can use each element and how that might map out over time.

- Prompt your students to use online discussion to compare approaches.
- Give them feedback, so that they can check their developing understanding of good practice.
- Prompt them to prepare for and organise their meetings.
- Build in an element of peer review of work-in-progress and of final presentations.
- Take a didactic role, for example, point out the minimum font for slides, the maximum number of slides for the length of their presentations, etc.
- Align their presentation activity with the learning outcomes and criteria and/or prompt them to do so. What are the criteria for the presentations? If there are none, consider developing some that are aligned.
- Refer them to a specific page, such as 'Pruning style/Keywords', and start a discussion about the reasons for 'pruning', about what is lost in the process, if anything, or about the concept of 'visual writing'.
- In case they miss it, point out that there is important 'technical information' on this site. This can help them sort out problems with the software.
- Check that they understand what 'parallelism' means for their own writing of slides. Can they give you an example from their presentations? Can you give them another from one of yours?
- Summarise discussion and point out where there is consensus – and continuing debate – about certain aspects of presentation practice. Where there is consensus, you may feel you can get the group to agree that this is now a requirement for all presentations. Where there is disagreement, you may have to take a stand on one side or the other, or point out that debate and dialogue are inevitable and useful (Mann, 2005). Or perhaps each student has a choice to make for his or her presentation. It will be helpful to spell this out – where they have choice and what the options are.
- If your students have poster presentations to prepare, point them to another resource on the same website, but spell out to them how they might use it, if you have time. As with the other sites, clarify the extent to which these sites – or others? – set the standard for presentations.

In practice, from the student perspective, e-learning will probably combine interactive and non-interactive resources. As e-tutor, you can help students integrate the whole thing, all forms of learning: prompting them to find more information than you have, to find alternative evidence for your points, to find counter-arguments, both established and original, to the material you – or others – present to them. You can prompt students – to suggest ways in which they can retrieve, select and use information and to share their views of different sites.

In order to do this, you have to know what they are doing, and, while it might seem a simplistic approach, it is probably essential simply to ask them, from time to time, how they performed their learning tasks, what they do at each stage and whether they think what they are doing is, in any sense, in their eyes, 'working'. Instead of feeling that you have to help them make all the connections, you can ask them how they see it. So that this type of discussion does not degenerate into a 'complaints' session, you can post questions for the group to discuss.

Making connections in e-learning

Connections can be made:

- between what you hear in the lectures on this course;
- and what you have found on the web;
- with what you hear from each other in discussions;
- and what you read in the course textbook;
- with your prior knowledge on other courses;
- to your own experience;
- and to the course's learning outcomes.

Where are the connections? Which connections do they see? When you prompt them to discuss these with each other, they can compare their answers. You could facilitate this learning, consolidation or revision moment as a short discussion, a short writing task or a discussion topic.

In this way, you not only make their learning the subject of discussion – including the content and curriculum – but also gain insights into their e-learning, as do they. On the basis of these insights, you can make suggestions about how they can improve their e-learning. An added advantage of such discussion is, of course, that they learn from each other.

Students also respond well, in general, when you draw on your own experience: how you prepared your first essay, your first lab report, your first presentation, and what you learned from that experience. You can talk about what you found difficult when you did this or a similar course. Describe how you managed to find a way through this difficulty. Then bring discussion back to the proposed topic for discussion.

For online learning to occur – as in face-to-face learning – students have to be able to voice their misunderstandings, partial understandings and doubts. It is your role to make sure that when this happens, the response is positive. With electronic discussion, students have longer to think about things than in face-to-face labs or tutorials. You have to develop a collection of prompts that ensures students think, and keeps the contributions coming. The strategies covered in the previous chapter will be a good starting point for you.

Portfolio

[Information and computer technology] can help students to learn more effectively. (Nomdo, 2004: 205)

For all the similarities with other forms of teaching, many see e-learning as a completely new area, a new form of teaching that brings opportunities for new types of learning. Whilst we are aware of all our warnings about overinvestment when you have a research project to finish, here is an example of an opportunity you may take to demonstrate special achievement in your portfolio. Think carefully about what you can and cannot do, however.

There might be scope here for you to demonstrate innovation and assess its impact. There might be funding for small projects. This might be an area worth watching and actively developing. There may be colleagues who are particularly interested in e-learning in your institution. They may be delighted to have an extra pair of hands on their projects.

If you go down that road, you need to consider precisely how your work is innovative, since there is a school of thought that says e-learning is not innovative but routine in the twenty-first century.

However, an equally important project would be to show how you bring the skills of 'traditional' teaching to e-learning. If you can demonstrate that any of these is successful in improving learning, you will be very popular. You may even find that simply finding a way to make e-learning work attracts attention in itself.

Demonstrating evidence of impact, however, such as establishing that there is a causal relationship between what you did in your teaching and what your students learned as a result, is difficult; there are so many variables and no control group (Means and Haertel, 2004: 12–17). Even available alternatives to the experimental approach must have rigour in their design, and this may be beyond you at this point in your career: there simply may not be time for you to read up on and develop this expertise at this time. The point of mentioning all of this here is to prevent you from claiming an effect that you cannot evidence.

Whatever your level of skill, presumably you will be learning from your own observations of student uptake of e-learning, their behaviours and, above all, their performance: notice what is different, if anything, about the way they interact with you or with each other, the way they work and perform tasks. Observations you can make include: are students solving problems in different ways, or more quickly? How do you and they see interactions in this forum? How do you measure e-learning? One study has shown that three groups performed the same task in very different ways: two groups moved through 'discussion' and 'negotiation' to 'work' and 'production', while the third experienced 'leadership struggles', 'anxiety', 'closedness', and 'learning conflict' (McConnell, 2005). As with face-to-face groups, this may have little to do with your teaching and more to do with the group dynamic. Or does it?

Make your own judgement about e-learning: what are the capabilities and limitations of IT in your discipline as you see it at this stage?

What you can and should do is some systematic reflection, preferably perhaps, at this stage in your career, in collaboration with someone else. If you can get a more experienced colleague to guide you, you can begin to explore e-learning in terms of your own development as a teacher:

- the rationale for e-learning;
- the way in which you used it;
- what it seemed to mean to students;
- what you observed;
- how your students responded;
- what you think you can learn from the experience.

Can you collect extracts or transcripts of your interactions or interventions as an e-tutor? Do you need permissions to do this? Alternatively, can you summarise the way you played your role?

If you want to know more about this area, there is plenty of material out there. For example, Mark Russell developed a means of tracking student attendance in e-learning, while also providing assessment tasks and feedback for first-year engineering students (www.heacademy.ac.uk/e-tutor). Many such innovators are keen to share and collaborate.

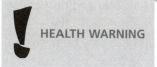

HEALTH WARNING Are you really expected to be innovative as a postgraduate tutor? Do you even have the freedom to do that? Even if you have formal responsibilities, such as module coordinator, you may have little freedom to innovate. You should check.

You may also not have the time.

Once you have mastered the basics – or more than the basics – of e-learning, you may find that you are seen as an expert. You may be invited to train other tutors. See if you can get some training for this role (if you feel that you need it), some support and, as always, a clear definition of your role. If the last of these is not provided, you can draw up your own remit: write a statement of what you can and cannot provide, and give it to your 'trainees'. Your work in this role will, of course, be useful for your portfolio.

Finally, collect commendations. As students or peer 'trainees' report that they found something you said or did in the e-learning environment was particularly useful, copy and paste the comment into a file for your portfolio.

Additional resources

Berge, Z. 'The role of the online instructor/facilitator'. http://www.emoderators.com/moderators.

JISC InfoNet. 'Effective use of virtual learning environments (VLEs)'. http://www.jiscinfonet.ac.uk/InfoKits/effective-use-of-VLEs.

Salmon, G. 'The five step model: Certified e-learning Professional (CeLP) Programme'. http://www.elearningprofessional.com.

Deazley, R. and Boardman, K. (2003) 'Biting the bulletin: embedding a culture of online learning in law'. http://www.ukcle.ac.uk/ict/durham.html.

Anderson, T., Rourke, L., Garrison, D.R. and Archer, W. (2001) 'Assessing teaching presence in a computer conferencing context', *Journal of Asynchronous Learning Networks*, 5 (2). http://www. sloan-c.org/publications/jaln/v5n2/v5n2anderson.asp.

Garrison, D.R., Anderson, T. and Archer, W. (2001) 'Critical thinking and computer conferencing: a model and tool to assess cognitive presence', *American Journal of Distance Education*, 15 (1): 7–23. http://www.communitiesofinquiry.com/documents/CogPresFinal.pdf.

Your First Laboratory or Fieldwork Practicals

I think laboratory teaching will be interesting, maybe even fun, but I'm not too sure I'll be able to answer detailed questions about these experiments, and I've never marked lab reports before.

Laboratory investigation is integral to the physical and biological sciences, such as physics, chemistry, geology and biology, and to all forms of engineering. However, practical work is also essential in many other disciplines, such as health-related areas (e.g. physiotherapy, nursing, medicine) and other subjects such as social sciences, psychology and the arts (e.g. fine art).

Field visits have been common in the sciences, particularly 'outdoors' subjects such as geography, biology, archaeology and agriculture. Field trips to building or industrial sites may be included in the curriculum for engineers and architects, historians may take a trip to battlegrounds, and medics or allied health professionals may visit clinical or community health care organisations.

Normally the term 'practical classes' refers to investigative or experimental work that students undertake in laboratories or in the field, and you may know from your own experience that postgraduates, often called demonstrators or instructors, frequently teach these classes. You should be well placed to engage in and enjoy this type of teaching, since you may be deeply immersed in doing research, using similar skills and techniques to your students.

Practical classes should stimulate interest and present opportunities for your students to see how subject knowledge has been generated by investigation, experimentation and systematic enquiry. They should also develop the technical and manipulative skills associated with the discipline, as well as cognitive skills such as problem definition, problem-solving and analysis. Furthermore, practicals are ideal situations for your students to refine their teamwork skills, since much of this work is done in groups. Importantly, these activities help them to understand and develop the attitudes of the discipline-based professional.

In writing this chapter, we have tried to focus on topics and issues which will be of interest and use to postgraduates teaching in all subject areas. Since the language of various disciplines may vary, we use the terms 'laboratory' and 'fieldwork' throughout, hoping you can adapt the principles to your discipline.

We begin with a discussion of role, followed by a longer section which deals with responsibilities, key principles and actions. This reflects the complex and serious nature of organising and facilitating experimental and investigative study. In particular, we deal in some detail with issues of health and safety. We also focus on the strategies that you can use to develop your students' thinking skills through the craft of listening and questioning, where the laboratory provides an excellent environment for postgraduates to enter into discussion with individuals or small teams of students. At the end of this chapter, we point out the specific differences between laboratory and field studies. Lastly, we suggest ways in which you can collect further evidence for your teaching portfolio.

What is your role?

Postgraduates tell us that their involvement in teaching laboratory and fieldwork varies, and can range across:

- having sole responsibility for running laboratory or fieldwork sessions and marking all laboratory or field reports;
- demonstrating in conjunction with a member of staff and sharing marking;
- participating in only one or two laboratory sessions, with no marking responsibilities.

Normally, postgraduates say they do not actually design the practical work; this is done by academic staff in conjunction with technicians. Occasionally, postgraduates have been asked to pilot an experiment that is subsequently adopted for an undergraduate class. As with all other teaching functions, you will need to clarify exactly what your role is by discussing this with the module coordinator or course leader.

As a demonstrator you will be giving instructions and explanations to the whole class and then letting students work, individually or in groups, on an experiment. This means that you will be using some of the skills you need for lecturing and facilitating group learning. Certainly, you will want to generate interest and enthusiasm, give clear instructions, ask questions and listen attentively to answers, observe body language, and judge when to exercise control and when to allow freedom.

Our postgraduates say that facilitating laboratory and fieldwork can be a really rewarding experience because they are able to guide and encourage students as individuals. Because you are likely to be closer to the students in age and experience, you may be seen as more approachable. You can assist students at all stages of their experimental work. One of the real 'perks' of teaching practicals is the opportunity to get to know individual students and engage in one-to-one dialogue about the subject matter. This can be very satisfying since you will have more time for crafting questions to guide your students' learning, and you may be able to see them develop their understanding.

What will you need to do?

Whatever the level and extent of your involvement with practicals, there are some responsibilities you will almost certainly have, and these require particular skills.

Preparation

You will need to know the broad aims and learning outcomes, as stated in the module descriptor or outline, so that you see the big picture and have a 'feel' for how the practicals develop or can reinforce learning. The general aims of practicals are similar, regardless of subject (Allison, 1995; Boud et al., 1986; Brown and Atkins, 1988; Stenglehofen, 1993).

General aims of practical work

- Illustrate principles taught elsewhere and consolidate knowledge.
- Practise discipline-related methods and procedures.
- Develop technical skills associated with the discipline.
- Develop cognitive skills such as critical awareness, systematic enquiry and observation, problem-solving, and analysis and interpretation of data.
- Bridge theory and practice.
- Enhance teamworking skills.
- Develop professional skills and attitudes.

Subject knowledge can be very complex and, often, abstract. Students can be enabled to consolidate and apply their knowledge through experiments that illustrate principles and theory taught in lectures: by communicating in the technical language of the discipline; by seeing and handling the materials and/or organisms they have been reading about. The hands-on experience that students get in the laboratory is crucial to the development of their technical skills and their understanding of the discipline-specific methods and procedures. They use the apparatus and tools, practise manual dexterity, and learn the discipline of careful observation, recording and report writing.

In performing experiments, students also develop a range of thinking skills necessary for defining and analysing problems, classifying and interpreting data and drawing conclusions, and they can learn how experiments can be set up to solve problems. The cooperative nature of these activities can promote students' teamwork skills as, together, they design and set up experiments, collect data, discuss results and write reports.

Collectively, the development of all these attributes can help students to appreciate the discourse of the discipline and approaches to enquiry. Development of professional attitudes is a more subtle and perhaps more long term goal.

What are the aims and learning outcomes of the practical work you will be facilitating? In addition to the broad aims of the module or course, there should be specific aims and learning outcomes for each of the practical exercises. If they are not clearly stated, ask the lecturer responsible. After all, if you do not know the purpose of the practical, it is possible the students will not either. And it will probably be your task to ensure students understand why they are carrying out the experiment.

You also need to know how students will be assessed on their practical work. What are the assessment tasks and the criteria? What is the lecturer looking for? As with all teaching, ask whether the learning outcomes, assessments and practical tasks are aligned. If they are not, try to discuss this with the tutor. Rehearse with him or her how you will help students relate the activity to the assessment.

What method or approach is being used? There are numerous alternative strategies for practicals, so you have to talk through this with the lecturer or course leader. Here are a few examples of alternative approaches (adapted from Brown and Atkins, 1988).

Exercises   These are tightly structured experiments with precise instructions which are useful for teaching observation and manipulative skills.

Structured enquiry   These loosely structured experiments require students to develop procedures and/or give their own interpretations of results. They teach manual, observational, problem-solving and analytical skills.

Open-ended enquiry   Students identify and formulate a problem, develop procedures, interpret results and discuss their implications and, in doing so, use many of the skills necessary for research.

Projects   Projects involve long experiments, field studies or a series of experiments which may be carried out individually or in small groups. They develop research skills, initiative and independence; they are stimulating, deeply engaging and valued by students.

PSI (personalised system of instruction) or Keller plan   Students pursue study at their own pace using do-it-yourself instructions; mentors or proctors (students who have completed the course) provide support.

Audio-tutorial   This method makes use of audio and perhaps video cassettes or CD-ROMs, printed material and simple apparatus. Lectures and tutorials may be optional.

Computer simulation   Experiments are simulated, with possibilities to vary parameters and conditions. Students are asked to process data, and may be presented with different scenarios. These are useful when cost, time and/or complexity prevent direct experimentation and are becoming more common.

Integrated laboratory   Several disciplines may be integrated to form a common laboratory programme, such as physiology, pharmacology and biochemistry.

Organising and planning

It may be that all the background work, such as experimental design, testing and planning, has already been done by academic staff, and all you need to do is prepare to assist on the day. However, you may be given the laboratory manual and asked to organise individual laboratory sessions. If this is the case, you should engage in careful planning, forward thinking, good communication with technicians and attention to detail. You will know from your own experience how easily experimental work can go wrong because of problems with equipment, reagents and/or logistics. Technicians will need to be contacted well in advance to ensure everything is ready on time. Remember that samples, live organisms and reagents take time to prepare, and although the lecturers may well have put in their orders, check it. Take time to talk to the technicians about your plans; they are a goldmine of information and an essential part of the team that supports experimental work. The following questions are meant as an *aide-mémoire* for your planning:

- Will all reagents and materials be available in adequate quantities?
- Will enough of the necessary equipment be available and functioning properly?
- Will there be enough glassware and disposable supplies?

- Will the appropriate accessories, such as cuvettes or special containers, be available in enough quantity?
- Can specimens, samples or live organisms be supplied on the day in adequate quantities?
- Should you prepare and copy instructions for students, or do they have everything they need in a laboratory manual? Do they all have copies of the manual? You may wish to add some of your own notes, diagrams or illustrations.

Of course, none of this may be your responsibility since it may have been done by another member of the teaching team. But if you are uncertain, ask.

Understand the experiment

Whatever the level of involvement you have, understand the experiment. Know how to do it, what the results are and how the experiment should be written up. For a start, this will help you to organise for your students, since you will have to arrange for all materials in advance. Furthermore, if you know the experiment, you should also be able to anticipate areas of difficulty and will therefore be ready to help students if they get stuck. This is probably the most important of your responsibilities because of the complex nature of practical work. If you think about it, students will need to interpret and follow instructions, set up and use apparatus (noting whether it works properly), make observations, collect and record results, calculate and analyse results, record any usual circumstances which might affect method or results, formulate conclusions and then write it all up. If they have a pro forma to use, you will have to get to know that too.

On the day

As you meet your students for their (and your) first laboratory practical, you'll have a number of things to achieve. Arrive early. Take attendance if you have been asked to do so. Students should have been told in advance that they need to purchase protective clothing, so you should make sure they have it. For the very first laboratory period, most departments have spare lab coats for those students who have been unable to acquire one. However, you should instruct them to get one by the next period, suggesting a nearby supplier. The next topic to deal with is health and safety.

Health and safety

It will be paramount that your students understand health and safety regulations for working in the laboratory. As a postgraduate, your own research and training will mean you know much of this information already. However, do not assume your students have read the regulations in their laboratory manual or handbook. Talk to them about safety, reiterating the main points, such as rules about clothing, eye protection, eating and drinking. Walk them through what they should do in the event of an accident or a fire and show them where the safety equipment is located. Point out the fire exits if they do not already know where they are. If there are specific routines that must be observed, talk them through the procedures. For example, where and how should they dispose of toxic wastes, radioactive materials or sharp disposables such as needles and blades? Explain where particular chemicals or equipment are stored and why the storage is organised in the way it is, so that they will understand the rationale.

Typical health and safety regulations

- Protective clothing, such as a lab coat, is mandatory.
- Protective eyewear is mandatory.
- No eating or drinking in the laboratory.
- Disposable gloves should be worn when handling hazardous, dangerous or radioactive substances.
- Pipetting by mouth is forbidden.
- Hazardous waste must be disposed of as instructed.
- Volatile substances must be decanted under an extraction hood.
- Decanting radioactive substances must done behind a protective screen.

It will not be enough to say all this once. As students work, they will probably forget and may make mistakes. It is your responsibility to monitor their work and help them to develop safe habits. You need, always, to be alert to a potential accident or an action which could cause harm: for example, if a student starts to pour organic solvents down the drains or forgets to use ether under the extraction hood. Naturally, you should ensure you also set a good example by observing all health and safety rules yourself.

Importantly, you should think in advance about the potential for accidents. This applies to both general aspects of laboratory work and specific experiments. It is a good idea to think through how you would deal with an accident. Do you know who to contact immediately? Do you know the emergency phone number?

Do you know who the nearest health and safety officer is and how to contact them? Do you know who the nearest first aid officer is? Do you know the procedures for contacting a doctor or an ambulance? What if your class is held after normal working hours (evening): what should you do in these circumstances? Remember that if an accident happens, you may be in charge, and you need to remain calm and decisive.

If your students are using any chemical substances, you should know about the UK Regulations for the Control of Substances Hazardous to Health (COSHH), or their equivalent. All chemicals have a COSHH rating and there will be a set of files for all the chemicals used in your department. You should know where to get information and what procedures to follow in the case of an accident.

Ground rules

Of course, ground rules are closely linked to health and safety, since personal behaviour may affect the safety of others. Again, do not assume that students will have read the ground rules in the handbook or laboratory manual. Take the time to discuss these with them. It might even be helpful to start by asking the group what they think the ground rules ought to be. Typical ground rules might include:

- Behave courteously towards your classmates.
- Keep bench area tidy and uncluttered; clear up as you go.
- Discard glassware and disposables as instructed.
- Replace equipment and materials immediately after use.
- Raise your hand if you have a question and the demonstrator will come to you.
- Before leaving, clean bench area as instructed.

There will be important specific ground rules and codes of conduct for practicals which involve students, perhaps of different genders, physically touching each other and/or in various states of undress, such as when practising joint manipulation in physiotherapy. These rules and codes will have been set by academics on the basis of professional ethics, which students must embed in their practice, but it will be your responsibility to know and enforce them. Where you may have to deal with students from different cultural backgrounds, we advise that you discuss policy and process with experienced staff.

Giving instructions

Whatever your involvement with laboratory teaching, you are likely to be giving instructions about processes and procedures to the class as a whole as well as to individuals and groups of students as they work. At the beginning of the class, take time to review the aims and intended outcomes of the experiment in order to help students understand why they are undertaking the exercise. Then, briefly summarise the procedures, even though these may also appear in the laboratory manual. You can use this time to highlight the most important steps, caution about particular aspects of the procedure, and call attention to any changes or differences from the printed protocol. Of course, it is easy to say that instructions should be clear, logical and unambiguous, but less easy to do. Diagrams, flowcharts and decision trees may be necessary to support complicated instructions. Students may also wish to ask questions of clarification at this point. Be careful not to use up too much time giving instructions, as students usually need all the allocated time to set up, run the experiment, take notes and tidy up.

As students work, you should circulate round the room to answer questions and give any further instructions students may need. You may find that students whose first language is not English will ask for further interpretation of the written instructions. By observing your students' body language you may be able to determine whether they are having difficulty. Students who are shy or unconfident may not ask for help.

Asking and responding to questions

Demonstrating gives you an ideal opportunity to develop your skills of listening and questioning as a means of facilitating learning. Students sometimes ask questions to which you can respond with a straightforward factual answer:

Where will I find the sample cells for the spectrophotometer?

Would it be OK for us to move this water bath?

Could you please show me how to switch on this equipment?

Other questions may require a more thoughtful response. For example, students may not know how to interpret their results and may ask you to help. Telling them the answer will not encourage them to think for themselves. Instead, you may use a series of questions to guide their thinking. This means you may have to probe back to the point at which they stopped understanding and scaffold a series of questions to lead them to the correct conclusion. To do this, you can use, as appropriate, the types of questions we suggested in Chapter 3, but tailored to practical investigations.

Questioning strategies for practical work

Information seeking

- Could you please explain to me exactly what you did?
- What colour was the sample before you added X reagent?

Clarifying

- Do you think you may have made an error somewhere?
- Have you checked that your standard samples are reading correctly?
- Did you notice any irregularities in the data collected from this sample?

Elaborating

- Can you tell me any more about the irregularities you noticed?
- Is there any more information you know about this particular geographical area?

Reasoning/justifying

- What do you think could account for the results you see?
- How could the circumstances have affected the data you have collected?

Evaluation

- How do you know your data are accurate?
- What do you think these results mean?

Comparative

- Where have you seen samples (results) like these before?
- How do these results differ from what you were expecting?
- What might happen if we were to change one variable?

Opinion seeking

- What do you think you should do now?
- How would you solve that problem?

More probing questions

- Do you think that would always apply?
- What is the relevance of this?

- How reliable (complete) is the evidence?
- What is the underlying principle (concept/issue) then?
- Which particular kind of (rock, organism, reaction, arch, etc.) is this?

These kinds of questions can be usefully employed to guide thinking and reasoning. It may be necessary to start with information seeking or recall questions, summarise and then move on to more probing questions to encourage deeper learning. Sometimes prompts, which give hints, are helpful to guide the response, especially if the student seems to be 'stuck'.

In teaching physical or manipulative skills, you may need to use gestures or 'hands-on' demonstration as well as verbal prompting. So, you may say, 'This is the movement (touch) you should use here', as you show students what you mean.

Monitor progress

As you circulate around the room, systematically check on students' progress with the task. You can take this opportunity to give encouragement or praise and to correct small mistakes, such as incorrect (or absence of) units or incorrect technique. You will be summoned by individuals who need assistance, but you should try to attend to every student; do not spend too much time on any one person or group.

Moving among the students will allow you to ask open questions to see how well they understand the work. For example, 'You've got a good set of data there, what do you think would be the best way to plot it?' You can also be alert to body language; lack of eye contact or bent shoulders may mean a student is not getting on well and needs help. Or it may mean he or she is just concentrating.

If your students are working in groups and you are called over by one of them, speak to the whole group rather than the single student. Alternatively, if students are working alone and one is having difficulties, find out if others are experiencing similar problems and ask them to discuss it together. This strategy will encourage the group to solve the problem together.

Knowing when to help and when not to help is an art that can be learned through experience, but it relies on keen observation and sensitive responses. If you learn to anticipate and recognise major gaps in understanding, and perfect the art of asking questions, you could have a major impact on students' learning.

Summing up

Leave time at the end of the period to finish with a brief summary or review. Invite students to contribute and ask further questions to help them see the relationship between their work and the theory. If students are having difficulty understanding, you may need to talk through the experiment with diagrams and explanations. Modelling thinking may help them see where they have failed to make connections.

If students are to do any follow-up tasks, such as report writing, reading or preparation for next time, remind them, including any due dates they should know. Lastly, ensure your students leave the laboratory clean and tidy and that equipment is left in a safe state.

Marking

Like all other assessments, there should be defined criteria for students' laboratory and field reports. Within each discipline there are well established formats for reports and students must develop their abilities to write reports, according to expectations. Normally, there will be a form for you to use for marking and feedback, and the criteria should be listed there so that students can see how they have been marked. Like other types of assessments, when you are new to this kind of marking, it is a good idea to have an experienced staff member cross-mark some of your work.

Fieldwork

Benefits

Classes taken in the field can be wonderful and rewarding learning experiences for both students and postgraduates. Postgraduates tell us how much they value the advantages of field trips so that they can:

- Experience, first hand, the realities of professional, business, artistic, industrial or environmental problems: 'I had no idea how chaotic it could seem behind the scenes, with everyone rushing around like mad. But of course, it was organised chaos since everybody knew exactly what they had to do.'
- Appreciate how hard it may be to act as professional practitioner at work: 'That patient was so difficult. I couldn't imagine myself handling that situation so well and keeping my temper. What a star.'
- See, 'in the flesh', the phenomena that are being discussed in class: 'Wow! Those basalt pillars are fantastic! It makes you really think about the cooling rates and physical forces that were exerted on the molten lava. Why did it happen like that only in particular places in this same location?'

- Appreciate the difference between what happens in the controlled laboratory environment and the complexity of the field situation: 'The fluctuations in population were very different to those we observed in our lab experiments, even though the temperature ranges were the same.'
- Ask questions that would not have occurred to them otherwise: 'I see there are no limpets clinging to these rocks further round the shore here. Why do you think that is?'

If you are involved in field excursions, it will be an extra opportunity for you to learn more about your own discipline too. The informal atmosphere lends itself to creative and stimulating discussions with colleagues and students.

Specific issues

There are, of course, specific issues associated with field trips for you to think about:

- safety issues specifically associated with the location, such as industrial sites, weather changes or difficult terrain;
- logistics of organisation and transport;
- transport, management and operation of equipment;
- special arrangements for disabled students or students who, for a legitimate reason, are unable to participate fully.

Normally, more than one member of staff will be present on a field trip, and the lecturer will be one of them, so your role may be that of assistant. However, you may be asked to help organise and prepare for the excursion, and this is good experience. Planning and forward thinking are as important as the planning for a laboratory session. To help you think through this role, consider the following questions.

Organising field trips

- Do you need advance approval for field trips and, if so, from whom?
- How far in advance do you need to seek approval?
- Which site will you visit and where is it?
- Will you need to make a pre-visit and, if so, when and with whom?
- Whom should you contact to arrange the visit and confirm the details?
- When will you go and for how long?

- How many students will be going?
- How many staff will be going and who are they?
- Will there be any expert contributors and, if so, who?
- How will you travel and how do you make arrangements for that?
- Who will pay the travel expenses and what are the procedures for approval of travel arrangements?
- What equipment, including safety gear, do you need to take and who will organise that?
- Who will be responsible for pre-excursion briefing and instructions?
- Who will debrief students?

It may not be your job to organise all this, but you will need to know it in any case. If it is, partly or fully, your responsibility, you will need to start planning well in advance to make sure students can make the visit during the semester or term, and when it is suitable for others, such as lecturers, technicians, caretakers or managers.

Once you are in the field, remember that this is a very informal situation, and you may need to act as shepherd, taking occasional head counts, and checking that no one has wandered off or got lost. Do not depend on the lecturer, who will be concentrating on the subject and the teaching.

Postgraduate fears

The experiment doesn't work

Postgraduates tell us that they can remember when experiments failed during their undergraduate studies. It happens to everyone, so don't panic. If students do not get the expected results, discuss it with them and try to work out what went wrong. Have students checked their procedures? Did they do everything as instructed? Were your instructions accurate? Is the failure isolated to one group or has the whole class had a problem? If it is the former, another group may share their results so that at least everyone has data to analyse and report. Alternatively, you might record data sets from all the groups on the board and ask all students to use the collated data. If the whole class has failed to produce data, it may be best to provide data from former experiments (for example, from last year). Also, you will need to contact the lecturer and technician to see if you can solve the problem, or otherwise it may recur with the next class. Of course, this situation is less likely to happen in the field, where measurements of natural phenomena are being taken.

Equipment failure

Hopefully your laboratory will have several pieces of the same equipment, so that if one is faulty, students can use another. This may mean, of course, that they need to wait and their work is delayed. Alternatively, suggest that they join another group. In the meantime, don't try to repair equipment yourself; call the technician. Sometimes, apparent failure can be due to 'glitches' in a computer program or to students not following the instructed protocol.

Disruptive behaviour

It is uncommon for students to exhibit disruptive behaviour, but if they do, deal with it swiftly and firmly. Such circumstances may arise if a student has become disengaged because the work is too difficult or because he or she has already finished and is bored. Since you will have discussed and agreed ground rules at the beginning about wandering off, moving around the laboratory and idle chat, a quick reminder will probably suffice. If not, and if safety is at risk, you must act to stop the student's behaviour, even if it means asking the student to leave. Clearly, the staff who are in charge will have to be informed.

A preferable solution is to try and prevent disruptions from happening in the first place by planning ahead. If you have been carefully observing the students at work, you may have spotted the student who is struggling conceptually; offer some assistance, drawing in other members of the group, if appropriate. For those students who finish early, plan some additional, more challenging exercise to keep them busy.

Accidents

Again, forward thinking will help you to respond well to any accidents that may occur. During your planning stages, identify where and how accidents might happen and think through how you would deal with them. This will alert you to possible hazards and save you acting on impulse. This particularly applies if the UK COSHH (see above) Regulations (or equivalent) are relevant. Remember that your students will expect you to know what to do and will be looking to you for instructions. Know the evacuation procedures, and the contact numbers for first aid and technical staff. And you will have to record the accident in the accident book, probably held by the technician.

Student interactions

Because laboratory and field experiments are usually done in groups, there may be a situation when one student is not contributing to the task. Initially, talk to the group about what they are doing; ask the less involved student for an opinion and a summary of what his or her role is. You may also reassign tasks within the group. Make a note of the problem so that you can regroup students the next time.

Disputes between students in the laboratory or field happen rarely, and you should not get involved. Try to be observant and defuse tensions before they boil over. Focusing on the task at hand is an effective way to redirect students' attention.

We have mentioned above the issue of 'hands-on' touching between students, perhaps between genders. This should be dealt with by enforcing strict ground rules and professional codes of conduct from the beginning.

Evaluating your students' learning and your teaching

Practicals consume resources. They are expensive in terms of materials, equipment and staff time. They occupy a significant amount of students' study time, which includes writing up reports. As universities struggle with a shrinking unit of resource, alternative approaches to practical experiments are being tested, such as 'dry labs' and computer simulations. Already, departments are cutting back on laboratory work to save money.

In this context, it is even more important that we make the effort to evaluate students' learning from practical work, and that we seek constructive feedback. You can use some of the techniques we suggested for lectures and tutorials, such as the short quiz, the one-minute paper and the Post-it evaluation (see Chapters 2 and 10). Sometimes, the simple stem 'The most important thing I've learned from this experiment is ...' can be very revealing.

Day et al. (1998: 38) suggest a number of excellent and efficient strategies for evaluating your teaching based on seven key dimensions of practical work: equipment and facilities, health and safety, aims and design, preparation and briefing, interaction, assessment and monitoring. They present examples of pro formas which you can complete after each practical in order to collect wide-ranging feedback on these seven dimensions, or to acquire more general qualitative information on your teaching. These would serve as excellent sources of evidence for your portfolio.

Portfolio

Facilitating learning in the laboratory and field offers you new dimensions in investigating your practice. Instructing in these situations is complex and challenging, and the responsibilities can be exacting. Practical and field classes require good organisation, use of specialised equipment, materials and facilities, and attention to detail before, during and after class. Students will be seeking information, guidance and expertise, and this must be given sensitively, but with the purpose of promoting learning and independent thinking.

How will you document your experiences? What might you use as evidence for your teaching portfolio?

If you are managing laboratory sessions over a period of time, say a semester or two, consider keeping a diary or log, in which you jot down notes during the laboratory session. Your notes could include your observations, as follows:

- How did students respond to your instructions?
- What sort of questions did they ask?
- What kinds of difficulties did you encounter, and how did you deal with them?
- What would you do just the same next time?
- What would you do differently?
- Would you change the experimental design for next year? Why and how?
- What have you learned?

Alternatively, you can adopt or adapt one of the pro formas suggested by Day et al. (1998). You could enter your comments onto a paper or electronic copy after each class to form a systematic account of your experiences.

Additional resources

Allison, I. (1995) 'Demonstrating', in F. Forster, D. Housell and S. Thompson (eds), *Tutoring and Demonstrating*. Sheffield: Centre for Teaching, Learning and Assessment, University of Edinburgh and Universities' and Colleges' Staff Development Agency (UCoSDA).

Assessment of and Feedback to Students

The thing I most worry about is assessment. How do you know what mark to give?

I was given a big pile of papers to mark and told to get on with it. It took me absolutely ages but I had to keep going because the marks were due in a week.

We suggest that you read this chapter no matter what your assessment responsibilities will be. Even if you know you have no role in assessment, you need to know how the students you are teaching will be assessed so that you know how to guide their learning. This means knowing not just what questions will be on the exam, but how students' answers to those questions will be marked. We discussed in Chapter 1 the importance of aligning learning outcomes, assessment and teaching strategies. This chapter will help you with that task.

Assessment can be quite threatening and is a high-stakes activity for both students and teachers (Gibbs, 1999). Perhaps you have negative memories of your own about an assessment experience – these do not easily fade. Alternatively, you might also have some positive memories of good assessments – these do not usually fade either. We know from research and our own backgrounds what powerful experiences assessments are and how long we remember them. They can give us confidence and pride if we do well, but if they go badly, for whatever reason, they can undermine confidence, destroy motivation or have other serious consequences (Rowntree, 1987; Heywood, 2000). Because assessment is such a powerful motivator, this is also a case for harnessing that power and using assessment as a positive tool for learning and receiving feedback (Gibbs, 1999). You may remember from your own experience an assessment which you found quite challenging and required hard work on your part, but the result was that you learned a lot from it. Assessment should be an opportunity for your students to learn.

If you are worried about how tricky assessment can be, that is probably an appropriate starting point. It is a complex dimension of learning and teaching. However, it is likely you will be asked to contribute to the assessment of students, since this is a time-consuming process and postgraduates tell us that staff are often looking for help with it. It is also likely that at some point in your career you will need to assess others' work.

The aim of this chapter is to help you understand the complexities of assessment so that you do not take it on naively. You may already know that assessment is a serious responsibility, yet it is important for you to know what exactly that responsibility involves. If you find that you are surrounded by experienced staff who know what assessment involves, you should be able to get quick responses to your questions.

What are the key principles of assessment?

Although we begin with a simple maths problem, this is a discussion that postgraduates in all disciplines say they find helpful in understanding what they will be doing when assessing students.

Please mark the following problem out of 10:

$$
\begin{array}{r}
1357 \\
\times \quad 25 \\
\hline
6685 \\
2714 \\
\hline
33725 \\
\hline
\end{array}
$$

What was your mark?

When we ask postgraduates to mark this problem, the answers they give vary between 0/10 and 8/10. This is obviously a big spread of marks for the same piece of work. The rationales that we receive for these marks include the following statements:

The answer is wrong so it gets a zero. That's it, no argument.

Well, the student obviously knew how to do long multiplication but just made two careless errors, so I gave him 8/10.

I worked out that there were three main processes, two multiplications and one addition. Because the student made errors in two of those processes, I gave him 6/10.

The student made two mistakes, but didn't put a place-holder in the units column, so I deducted 3 marks from a total of 10 to give 7.

Well, the problem is wrong, but I thought the student made a good effort and I didn't want to demotivate him, so I gave him 5/10.

I just gave 3/10 for effort, but basically it's wrong.

How did you mark that problem and what was your reason?

It is easy to see there are several issues arising from this scenario. The wide range of marks for the same piece of work is one difficulty. Additionally, the variability in rationales indicates that each marker is in a situation where they are working from their own rules.

Context, validity and reliability

The problem with this scenario, of course, is that nothing is known about the context. Who are the students? What are they being tested on – in other words, what are the learning outcomes? What level of study are they engaged in? What is the subject area? These questions lead us to a discussion of a key concept relating to assessment: learning and assessment need to be constructively aligned. This means that the assessment must allow us to assess students' achievement of the learning outcomes. The associated criteria will define what the marker will be looking for in the assessment.

If this problem were part of a primary school test, for example, the learning outcomes might be that pupils should demonstrate ability to carry out long multiplication, showing all their work and presenting the problems in a neat and orderly way. The associated criteria might therefore include: all steps in the multiplication are shown; the problem is neatly and appropriately laid out on paper; the answer is accurate to within 10%. So a pupil submitting the problem above might be given 6 or 7 out of 10. These criteria are aligned with the learning outcomes, but do not severely punish a pupil who is still learning about mathematical processes.

On the other hand, if the problem were part of a third-year pharmacy exam, where students are required to demonstrate they can calculate drug dosages accurately, the criteria would emphasise the importance of accuracy and units of measurement, and the student would get 0/10. At this level of study, in this subject area, 100% accuracy is demanded and would be expected of students with considerable experience of mathematical calculations.

The term applied to this alignment between assessment and learning outcomes is *validity*. Validity is the degree to which the assessment tests the learning outcome(s). Put another way, a valid assessment allows students to demonstrate they have met the learning outcome. A helpful image to illustrate this point is to think of a valid assessment as being on target, like an arrow hitting a bull's-eye.

The other key term relating to assessment is *reliability*, which refers to reproducibility of marks. A reliable assessment is one which, when marked by several people, receives similar marks. A helpful image here is the set of marks given to a competitive skater or diver by a panel of judges during a major sports competition. Most of us would question a set of marks which ranged from 10/10 to 3/10. On the other hand, a reliable test might give the following set of marks, where there is some variation, but where most are clustered: 6, 7, 6, 8, 5, 6, 7, 7, 6, 7. Although postgraduates may not use the term 'reliability', they do regularly ask or express anxiety about whether they will be able to give the 'same marks' as an experienced lecturer. They are right to be concerned, as this is an important aspect of marking.

How do we make assessments reliable? Our discussion of the maths problem scenario above shows that markers tend to make their own rules about how to judge a piece of work, and of course this is very subjective. Therefore, we need a set of appropriate criteria, or guidelines, to help them make decisions about performance. Markers can then use the criteria when they mark each paper. Groups of teachers sharing the marking load will be using the same set of criteria to guide their decisions. Criteria are, therefore, important tools which lend objectivity to a subjective process, and can improve reliability of marking.

There is a second important reason for criteria, which is to inform students about how they will be judged. Criteria show students what it is that teachers value. It is, therefore, crucial that students know about and understand criteria. When they begin an assessment or piece of work, they will ask how they will be marked. What will the assessors be looking for? What elements of the work are important? What elements are less important? What level of quality are they aiming for? What standards are expected? In the past students had to rely on guesswork or trial and error to find answers to these questions. Perhaps you can remember trying to work out what your teachers meant by 'an academic essay' or 'a report' as you sat down to write. When you got your grade back, perhaps you were none the wiser about how to write a good essay or report or about the basis of your mark; this is no longer acceptable.

Students need to have, well in advance, information about how and when they will be assessed and what criteria will be used to judge their work. Assessment is not a guessing game; it is an opportunity for students to learn to respond to a clearly articulated remit with associated statements, or criteria, that tell them how they will be marked.

> ## Key features of criteria
>
> - Appropriate for context and learning outcomes.
> - Explicit and clear.
> - Achievable through the assessment task.
> - Known and understood by students in advance of the task.
> - Used as the basis for feedback to students.

A word of caution may be advisable here: even though you may be asked to mark assessments which have well written criteria, this may not be an easy task, and reliability will not be perfect. Do not expect that you can do a perfect job. We have to accept that assessment is a subjective process because we are human. However, the application of criteria or marking guidelines helps to remove some of the subjectivity in an effort to be as fair to students as possible. It is important that we do everything we can to improve objectivity and fairness. One way to improve your confidence in marking is to do marking practice with others, including those who have experience, and compare marks. This kind of practice is not always offered, though it is a sensible suggestion that you might want to make in your department or to a senior colleague.

Feedback

There is a third reason for criteria: to provide a framework for giving your students feedback. For each criterion, you have to make a decision about how well it has been met, and give the student a comment which explains that judgement. For example, you might give the following feedback to the school pupil who completed the maths problem above: 'You are coming on well with your long multiplication. I see you can multiply and add. Sometimes you make mistakes in carrying over units. It might help to put the number of units to be carried above the next column so you don't forget.' Notice that this feedback gives positive reinforcement to what is done correctly, points out errors and then gives constructive suggestions about how to do better next time. What feedback might be given to the third-year pharmacy student? What would be the most important point to make?

Your department should have procedures and pro formas for giving written feedback to students; if you are unaware of these you should ask. Many feedback pro formas include the assessment criteria, so that you can match your comments with each element of the criteria. Students frequently say this form of feedback makes the marking process more transparent and helps them to see why they have received the marks they have. You may also wish to give students feedback in the margins of their papers as a way of establishing a kind of dialogue with them. This can be an effective means of giving feedback, but some departments have reasons for not marking on the papers themselves. Ask about your department's policy.

Postgraduates tell us that feedback was one of the most important elements of their own learning, and we agree, and we say much more about feedback later in this chapter.

Standards

> **Standards:**   the level of achievement expected of students at any given stage in their education.

We have yet to mention the concept of standards. This is also an important term, and one you may hear frequently. Standards define the level of achievement expected of students at any given stage in their education. For example, what level of achievement is expected of a first-year student compared with a third-year student? What is the difference between the performance of third-year students at the University of Angst and third-year students at Butler's University? Are the achievements of history graduates at the University of Newby equivalent to those of Manner University College? In the UK, external examiners are charged with verifying that the standards of one university are equivalent to those in another. Their judgements are based on:

- level of learning outcomes;
- level of assessments and appropriateness of criteria;
- the institution's grade descriptors, which detail what level of performance is necessary to get an A or a C, a first-class or an upper second-class (2:1) degree;
- perusal of students' work in each grade band (A to F);
- the overall profile of class marks, e.g. percentage of fails and As or top classifications;
- feedback to students from staff;
- sometimes student vivas, as for honours projects.

In order to be transparent and fair to students, UK universities have well defined processes for assessment, marking, feedback and data handling. However, universities also have to present this information to external examiners, the verifiers of standards and assessment processes. External examiners also attend examination boards. These committees receive assessment data, make decisions about final grades or classifications, discuss problems associated with particular students and receive a report from the external examiner about standards of achievement. The external examiner will also comment on other aspects of the assessment process within your institution, such as validity and reliability of assessments, quality of feedback to students, turn-around time for marking, procedures for moderating and double-marking, and conduct of the examination board.

So why do you need know about standards? The first point to make here is that as a member of the teaching team in your department, you have a responsibility to support students' learning and achievement to, at least, the level that is expected of them. You may also be able to help your students understand what that standard of achievement is. The second point to make is that it has probably become apparent that, even if you never collate marks or attend examination board meetings, others will read coursework and examination papers. They will scrutinise both the marks and the feedback you have given your students.

Your role in assessment

In this section we want to deal with the possible roles you may have in assessing students. These may vary depending on institutional or departmental policies and practices, but there are a number of key questions you should be asking.

Defining your role in assessment

- What will you be expected to do: will you have to write assessments and criteria or just mark?
- How will you handle marking?
- Do you know what to do?
- What help will you get?
- What should you expect?

- What should you not tackle?
- How can you protect yourself?

Even if you are not involved in any assessment, you should know how the students you are teaching are going to be assessed so that you can ensure students have opportunities to engage with the subject matter and practise the necessary intellectual and practical skills.

Normally, assessment tasks are set by academic staff, and often this will be done at an early stage in planning for the academic session. The staff should also assign criteria for each assessment so that students can be given complete information about all their assessments early in the session. If this is the case in your department, you will not be required to design assessments, write instructions to students or write the assessment criteria. Your job may be to mark the work and to ensure that the learning and teaching experiences will allow students to prepare for their assessments. If you do find that you are asked to write assessments – or parts of assessments – and criteria, we advise you first to ask whether this should be your responsibility.

If you have established that you are expected to design assessments or to set exam questions and you feel anxious, seek assistance from the course leader or module coordinator and ask them to scrutinise your work, giving detailed feedback. Certainly, if you are in this situation, we advise you to read Chapter 1, and all of this chapter, as starting points. Other sources of useful information on assessment are to be found in Biggs (2003), Brown et al. (1997), Gibbs (1990; 1999) and Knight (1995).

What is more likely is that you will be asked to mark students' coursework or exam papers which have been set by someone else. What information do you need for this task and what questions should you ask? Our recommendations are given below; these questions will not change, regardless of the type of assessment being used.

Marking assessments set by someone else

- Who are the students?
- Which module or course are they on?

- What level or year of study?
- What learning outcomes are being tested by that assessment?
- What type of assessment is it and what instructions were given to students?
- What is the weighting of the assessment, e.g. how many marks will students get for this piece of work?
- What are the marking criteria?
- What have the students been told about feedback they will be given: when and how?
- What have you been told about giving feedback: when and how?
- What pro formas should you use to give feedback?
- What are the procedures for recording the feedback that you give to students: are you supposed to submit copies to a department administrator, for example?
- How much 'turn-around' time do you have in which to do the marking?
- Who do you give the marked papers to, and what tracking pro formas need to be attached?
- What are the policies and procedures about 'blind' double-marking, cross-marking or moderating? Do you know what these terms mean and which terms are used in your department?

Even when they have all the information they need, including criteria, what postgraduates often say is 'I still don't know what that means … I don't have the experience … I still don't know what constitutes an "A" or how to give it a mark.' The answer to that is, have you been given sample answers? Have you had any training, using past papers, for example, which are then cross-marked by an experienced member of staff? Has a more experienced member of staff agreed to cross-mark the papers you have been given? If not, then it is reasonable for you to have doubts about your readiness to be a marker. These are still the questions you should be asking. If you are inexperienced, have you asked if there's a staff development course that you could take?

This can be a difficult area: postgraduates often feel they have to do what they are asked to do. You may feel that you do not have the proper training or experience, do not agree in principle that you should be doing the marking, or do not see that assessments are aligned with learning outcomes and criteria. You may feel you do not have the credibility to mark the work of people who are as old as or older than you are and possibly more experienced than you are. You may not even have taught the course you are being asked to assess and do not know the content of the lectures, tutorials or lab discussions. You may be unsure about what students have or have not been told. You may feel like the 'meat in the sandwich'. You may feel you do not have the authority to say no. In fact, you may believe that you are the only one who feels this is not all straightforward, that it is your inexperience that is raising all these questions. You may feel unprepared to raise such questions; you may not understand the answers you get and may continue to feel the pressure of power relationships. Yet, you feel that you have to do what you have been asked to do. There is, after all, the power balance of postgraduates to supervisors and lecturing staff.

These are all common sources of anxiety which postgraduates express about assessing other students. The best way of dealing with them is to ask questions, clarify your responsibilities, and ask for training, mentoring and support from experienced staff in your department and from centres for academic development. And there is another, more positive way to look at your position: because you are also a student, and perhaps recently an undergraduate student, you will be closer to the students' perspective. You may well have a positive contribution to make to revising and clarifying instructions to students, for example. You may be in a better position to see ambiguities in assessments and can make suggestions for improvement. You may be able to suggest that student assessments impose workloads that are unrealistic. Many departments will welcome your point of view, acknowledging the value of your perspective.

Assessing different types of activity

You are bound to hear the terms 'summative assessment' and 'formative assessment' used by staff in your department. Although the generally accepted definitions are as shown in the box, there can be a blurring of the boundaries between formative and summative assessments. Students usually receive feedback on their summative assessments, such as presentations, essays, reports and creative works. Sometimes a formative assessment will form part of the overall summative assessment, for example, a project proposal might be worth 15% of the mark given for the project, but the student would get in-depth feedback on the proposal.

> **Summative assessment:** assessment which counts towards a mark, a grade, a classification and/or an award. It is usually used to measure performance during or at the end of a unit of study.
>
> **Formative assessment:** assessment designed to allow students to practise and receive constructive feedback to improve their knowledge and skills. Formative assessment often does not 'count' towards a final mark or grade.

The assessment principles discussed in this chapter – validity, reliability, standards – all apply to both summative and formative assessments.

Students can be assessed in different ways, many of which may be familiar to you. Because examinations are a common type of assessment in all universities, you are very likely to be asked to help mark exam papers. Exams which are made up only of multiple choice questions will be pretty straightforward to mark – and may even be marked electronically – but often exams include short answer questions, short essay questions and problem-solving questions which must be marked by hand. How will you go about doing that? What criteria do you have? Have you been provided with sample answers or a set of topics/ideas which should appear in the 'best' answer? What is the departmental policy about giving feedback on examinations? Some departments do and some don't, so you need to ask the question.

Other types of assessments include presentations, posters, essays, seminar discussions, reports, proposals, reflective accounts, learning logs, skills-based assessments, productions and creative works. It is probably fair to say that marking some types of assessments is less easy than others because of the latitude for subjectivity. For example, there has been discussion lately about portfolios, an assessment method which allows students freedom of choice about how to structure, what to put in, what to select out, how to organise and present. In this case, criteria need to be carefully thought out in order to accommodate this flexibility.

However, whatever the approach to assessment, the fundamental principles are the same. The assessment must be valid and reliable, and therefore you must know the answers to all the questions given above, and you must have a set of criteria. What may differ is the way in which you give feedback (oral and/or written) and the time it will take to do the marking. Generally, marking coursework is more time-consuming than marking examination papers. However, marking posters may take less time than marking essays. Ask members of staff and more experienced postgraduate teachers to help you estimate your time commitments and plan your work.

Peer assessment

Although peer assessment, or peer evaluation, is a fairly common activity in the working world, students at university often feel uncomfortable when asked to peer assess a fellow student. Reasons for this vary: they may feel it is the job of the staff, not themselves, to measure performance; they may feel ill-equipped, untrained and uninformed about how to do it; they may feel very awkward about judging people they know well, live with or socialise with. Even some postgraduates, when asked if they would like to peer assess each other's presentations or research proposals, are reluctant to do so. However, peer assessment can be a valuable learning experience, in that students have the (rare) opportunity to see or hear what others write or say. By using criteria to judge others' work, they can come to a much deeper understanding of how criteria can inform the development of a piece of work. They can also more fully understand the marking processes and see how staff go about marking work. If you have already done some marking, you may have realised these things yourself.

A number of universities are implementing peer assessment in different ways and to different degrees. Sometimes it is used for formative assessment only, providing an excellent opportunity for students to give and receive feedback. If used in a summative way, it is common for peer assessed marks to be amalgamated with the tutor's marks. One of the reasons for this is that both students and staff worry that peer assessment will not be reliable. In fact, research has demonstrated that with good criteria, students give marks that are very close to the marks awarded by staff (Falchikov, 2001). If you are asked to facilitate peer assessments, ask some questions first:

- Has 'this kind' of peer assessment been used before?
- Have ground rules, instructions and criteria already been established?
- Is peer assessment to be formative or summative?
- What percentage of the overall mark will be attributed to peer assessment?
- Have students been briefed about the process and do they know why they are being peer assessed?
- What is your role?

Self-assessment

Your students may feel more comfortable with self-assessment, which is – and perhaps should be – becoming a more common form of assessment in university and may be tied in with personal development planning (PDP) or personal development portfolios (Boud, 2000; Yorke, 2003). This, too, is a work-related type of assessment since many employers use this approach to professional development and/or appraisal. Many students have found that self-assessment is a rewarding process, enabling them to learn about themselves and evaluate their own performance against a set of standards (Boud, 1986; McDonald and Boud, 2003).

Using formative assessment

Formative assessments are intended to provide constructive feedback to students on their performance, to enhance their learning and help them understand standards of academic work (Juwah et al., 2004). The feedback should be given early in their course or programme, so that they have time to act on it. It is meant to be developmental and therefore does not 'count' towards a grade or mark. It is meant to give students the chance to practise and refine, to produce and modify. A typical formative assessment might be a draft short story, essay or report for which the student receives written (and/or oral) feedback and then uses those comments to rewrite it.

One of the problems with formative assessments is that students, whose time for study may be limited, do not always fully engage with them because they do not 'count'. One solution to this problem is to build formative assessment and feedback into summative assessment, so that the whole process becomes an integrated learning experience. A good example is the one above, where students are summatively assessed on the final copy of the story, but are given formative feedback on the draft. The whole assessment process becomes a learning experience about how to draft, critique, revise, receive critical feedback, revise, reflect, revise again, know when to stop writing, polish and submit. In our experience, it is rare that formative and summative assessment are so carefully integrated as to provide good learning opportunities for students. Do not be shocked if this is what you find, but work towards as much integration as you can.

Giving students good feedback

Research in learning and teaching has shown that feedback is probably the most significant activity for enabling learning (Black and William, 1998). Why? If you have had music lessons or sports coaching, think about the feedback you got. What did it tell you? How did it help you? What was important about the way it was presented to you?

Did your answers include some of the points below? Here are the characteristics of good feedback. It should:

- be timely;
- compliment what was done well;
- commenting on what was not done quite so well;
- give constructive advice about how to improve;
- be specific, that is, any comments or advice are detailed enough to be clearly understood.

Because research so clearly tells us how important feedback is for learning, we would like to say a bit more.

Be prompt   Try to return work and feedback as soon as possible after students have completed the assessment. The more time elapses, the less effective the feedback is, because students will have more difficulty remembering what they did and therefore will not be able to relate your feedback to their work.

Be positive as well as negative   Try to find something positive to say about a student's work. This is usually not problematic. You may compliment the structure or the evidence of wide reading or areas where the student has exhibited original or creative thinking, for example, 'You've taken an unusual perspective on this debate and made a good start at defending your point of view.' When giving feedback on what has not been done well, try to phrase it in a positive way, for example, 'I think you could have strengthened your argument at this point by referring to the research of Bassett and Wold (1999)', or 'Alternative solutions to problems like this are addressed by Coker and Shields. Do you think you should have made reference to these authors in your discussion?'

Because students tend to remember your negative comments and not the positive ones, avoid linking the two in a single sentence with 'but'. So, for instance, instead of saying, 'You have set out a suitable structure for your report, but your data do not justify your conclusions', put these remarks into two separate sentences.

Be constructive and specific   Feedback should be specific enough to tell students exactly what they need to do to improve their work. Comments like 'good' or 'well done' may make the student happy, but do not say what makes the work good or why you thought it was well done. A more helpful statement would be, 'Your introduction succinctly sets out what your paper will cover and the order in which you intend to do that.' If you say something is not good, is it because the student has, for example:

- got the data/information wrong;
- got the data right but in the wrong place;

- got incomplete data;
- used references which are out of date;
- simply reproduced what was covered in lectures;
- left out crucial elements/evidence relevant to the argument;
- wandered off track;
- not answered the question?

This level of specificity in your feedback will help your students to understand what you value and what it is they need to do to make their work better. Clarity is important: research has shown that students often don't understand feedback (Chanock, 2000). The following examples of specific feedback explain further what we mean:

> **You construct your sentences well, using appropriate grammar and punctuation, all of which help the reader to understand what you are saying.**

> **You have included a number of current references as well as the older, well-respected and seminal works on this topic.**

> **You have begun to address the emergent debate on this topic. Because we are interested in what is happening now, next time try to focus more on that and less on the historical development.**

> **Your illustrations are nicely done. However, do you think they clarify or add to your thesis?**

> **Your conclusion is relevant, if brief. What you have not done is to state how your discussion relates to current practice and current regulations.**

Use dialogue   One really helpful way of giving feedback is to pose questions which engage students in a dialogue. This is particularly good for feedback on essays. 'Did you read the article about ...', 'Do you think it would have strengthened your argument if ...', 'Had you thought of ...?' Of course, some of these are rhetorical questions, but the point is to get the students to think, rather than to tell them what to do or what not to do, thus using the opportunity to stimulate learning.

Use visuals   Putting your feedback in a kind of thought bubble makes it less threatening and signals further thought in a visual form. If this seems like a feeble attempt to be 'cool', the point is to take away some of the 'scare factor' in order to make assessment less threatening. The aim is to prompt students to think about what you are saying to them.

Be honest Find ways of giving feedback which students will know is honest. If you think a point has been well made, say so in a way that indicates you mean it, but is not gushingly overdone: 'This work is a considerable improvement on your first essay. In particular, you have responded to my earlier remarks about the importance of citing relevant supportive evidence.' If you need to be critical, find a way to say so without being hurtful. For example, you could write, 'I think you may have made some assumptions in deciding which data sets to collect. One assumption seems to be … . Do you think there are any others?'

Be careful not to give too much feedback Too much feedback (for example, scribbles and comments all over the paper) can overwhelm students, particularly if there are lots of things to correct. The student will think, 'What's the point in even trying to fix this?' and may feel demotivated. Select two or three things which will help the student most and comment on those. Students generally find they can only address a few things at a time, but with your continued feedback and support, they can make good progress.

Before concluding this section, we should alert you to one other aspect of marking: matching feedback with marks. It is important to ensure consistency between your feedback comments and the marks you give. For example, if you have said that the work is an excellently documented account of something, don't give 48%. This example is an exaggeration, but it is not uncommon to see remarks like, 'Excellent piece of work; well done' on an assignment with a mark of 60%. If you are in doubt about this particular aspect of marking, revisit your institution's grade descriptors, which describe what standard of work merits A, B, C, etc. These descriptors should tell you which range of marks can be considered 'excellent', for example.

Management of assessment

Mark management

If you are marking assessments, make sure you know how the marks will be managed in your department. This will be especially pertinent if you have lots of papers to mark or if you are marking just a portion of the assessment and the papers will move on to other markers. Management and recording of marks are part of university quality assurance mechanisms, but experienced staff sometimes forget to explain the process. If you do not know, ask:

- How are the marks to be calculated?
- Who is responsible for those calculations?
- How are the marks or grades to be recorded?
- Who is responsible for confirming the final mark?
- Who should you report your marks to?
- Are there any forms or computer databases that you should use to record your marks?
- What kind of records or tracking forms should accompany the marks?
- Who should you give the assessments to when you have finished marking?

Time management

Marking is time-consuming. Marking and giving good feedback are even more time-consuming, so this activity will need to be planned into your own research agenda. Marking and giving feedback on a 3000-word essay, for example, can easily take 30 minutes. What if you have 30 to mark? Or 50? Or 100? Or more? In order to manage your time, you need to know when assessments are due so that you can clear time for them. Remember that feedback needs to be timely, so the quicker you can turn around the marking, the better for students. You may also be working to administrative deadlines which require marks to be submitted to examination boards in, for example, three weeks' time. You may have less time if some or all of your papers need to be checked or moderated by another person. In that case, you will have to get them all finished to allow time for that step. If you are new to marking, you will probably want to ask that someone double-marks at least a sample of your papers, to give you confidence that you have done a good job and that your marks are in line with those of an experienced marker.

It is also important to think about how many scripts you can mark in one sitting. Marking demands concentration and is therefore tiring. Your marking may become more variable when you are tired, bored or fed up, so plan breaks. Rest or do something else when you begin to feel fatigued.

Detecting and preventing plagiarism

Has there been lots of talk around your department lately about plagiarism? This is not a new phenomenon, of course, but wide and growing use of the web has created easy opportunities for individuals to use words that are not theirs. Before we heavily penalise students for plagiarism, it is important to ask some questions:

- Do all students know what we mean by plagiarism?
- Do all staff define plagiarism in the same way?
- How many unattributed words does it take to be classed as plagiarism?
- Do students know when they have plagiarised?
- Can they identify plagiarism in their own work?
- Why do students plagiarise?
- Do students always plagiarise deliberately, hoping to 'get away with it'?

These may be questions that are currently under debate at your university, since this is a 'hot topic'. You may find that there are not many clear answers, but it is important to engage in the discussion if you are involved in marking. Students will certainly want to know.

> **Plagiarism:** plagiarism is the deliberate use of someone else's work as your own, where 'work' can refer to oral or written words, music, art, dance, etc.

Know what the university says and does about plagiarism:

- What is the university policy on plagiarism or 'academic dishonesty'?
- What are the university regulations relating to plagiarism?
- What are students told about it and where is the information?
- Who can give support to students who are still learning about writing without plagiarising?
- How are cases of plagiarism handled in your department?
- Whose responsibility is it to deal with cases of plagiarism?
- Who should you report suspected plagiarism to?
- What responsibilities do you have for warning students about plagiarism?
- What support will you get if you have to report plagiarism?

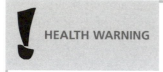

| HEALTH WARNING | Assessment is a major responsibility. Don't get out of your depth. Make sure you get all the information you need. Ask, ask, ask. |

Portfolio

What constitutes evidence of good practice in assessment and feedback? It is no longer good enough to say 'they all passed'. You need to provide evidence of what you did. But how do you make a causal connection between what you did and how the students did?

This is an excellent area to document your learning, as assessment is frequently an activity where postgraduates are not experienced. You may be on a steep learning curve here, so use the opportunity to keep a log of your learning.

- What were you asked to do?
- What were your initial concerns or doubts?
- What reading did you do?
- Who did you talk to about your concerns?
- Where did you go for information about policies, processes, regulations, student support, support for you?
- What training did you participate in?
- Did you organise for a mentor and, if so, how did that work for you?
- How did you handle any anxieties, pressure?
- What did you learn?
- What will you do differently next time and why?

You may have identified other general questions, or much more specific, perhaps discipline-specific, questions. Record your brief answers to them in writing. Go back to these answers and add later, developing thoughts and ideas. After you have done some marking, you may have new questions. You may have made mistakes. All of this can be recorded in your portfolio, and the process of recording is part of your own learning. Do not try to make this a continuous narrative at this point; instead, go back to it in six months' time and see what you notice. Your initial answers to these questions may be very different from your later answers.

Additional resources

Higher Education Academy. http://www.heacademy.ac.uk.

The HE Academy has a number of useful papers on various aspects of assessment.

Brown, G., Bull, J. and Pendlebury, M. (1997) *Assessing Student Learning in Higher Education*. London: Routledge.

A good place to start.

7

Student Relations

One of my students stopped me after the class to explain how difficult it was to keep up with the course because of problems. He asked me if I could give him some extra tutorials. Should I do that?

This is a crucial subject, since it concerns how you conduct yourself with students. You have to think about whether you should adapt your attitudes and behaviours in class, particularly face-to-face with students. Attitude and behaviour are a key part of your role as a tutor, since they can be so influential.

Your subject knowledge is the grounding for your role: what all parties expect is that you have relevant knowledge. However, you have to balance your subject knowledge with influencing social interactions and shaping the climate and motivations of students. You may feel that subject knowledge is most important and under threat, but your attitudes and behaviours are important too – some would argue more important. It is not just about your subject knowledge.

Set boundaries for yourself

Even when you are tutoring or lecturing, you are still a student. You are not a member of staff. Because of this, even when you have no formal role, undergraduates may approach you for support; they may see you as more approachable. What will you do? You could listen. You could refer them on. You could try and deal with their issues yourself. It is more questionable, but you may feel that you should advocate for a student. This may happen particularly with diversity issues. Watch out for signs of the Atlas complex in yourself: how much of the world are you going to take on your shoulders, given that you have been asked to do a fixed number of tutorials a year?

Questions for clarification

- What is your role?
- What are the ground rules?
- How long till it becomes someone else's role?
- What can you talk about?

- How responsible are you for students?
- How do you manage the power imbalance?
- What is your power?
- Is it the power of knowledge?
- Do you have the power of marking?
- Do you know how to enforce ground rules?

Listening, clarifying, interpreting.
How much time your role entails.
Can only spend so much time, then pass them on.
Subject related, not problem with flat mate interrupting study.
In subject area, not in their lives.

Superior knowledge of subject.
Knowledge of how university works.

Reminders, requests, warnings.

It is easier to state boundaries than to enforce them. It can be hard to say to someone that this is not anything to do with me, go and see someone else. It might be difficult to manage face-to-face. It might need time and practice to get it right. Just giving students a sympathetic starting point, and a name to go to, might be all they need. You can use a form of words that cues action or reflection.

- 'I may not be the best person to help you', 'The person who can help you is …', 'They can tell you precisely what is …'.
- 'It sounds to me as if it would be helpful for you to contact … services, and they will be able to help you.'
- 'What do you think would happen if … you were able to reduce the amount of time you currently spend stacking shelves in the supermarket … if you wrote the essay the way you are suggesting?'

Discuss all this in your department, but beware of general answers that encourage you to be 'sensitive' and 'responsive' to student needs. Of course, you will be sympathetic, but you also need to be clear about the limits of your expertise (and time).

Some student 'problems' might be educational issues that you think are part of your remit. Maybe not: there are other people whose job it is to be an advocate for students. There will be someone in your department who is responsible for addressing problems with courses. Postgraduates tell us that when students bring their problems to them, they frequently feel a strong sense of responsibility to do something to help. There is, of course, nothing inherently wrong with that, but the point is that you need to be clear about where the boundaries of your remit lie, and you must be prepared to tell your students where they are. There will be someone, or some group, in your department with this remit. Find out who they are.

What you can do is to encourage students to be their own advocates. If you come across students who feel that the world is against them, prompt them to use the rules, contacts and channels of communication to sort things out.

Undergraduates are trying to work out how to relate to you in this new environment; not all of them get this right, from the start. They are not sure where the boundaries lie. In addition, some may be vulnerable, or at least unsure of themselves, and may just ignore your boundaries. Some will not cope well immediately with independent study at university. You will have to be clear and consistent in these different situations about your boundaries.

Alternatively, you may find that the students you deal with are all mature. They might see you as being younger, relatively inexperienced and 'not a real teacher'. There is a potential role boundary issue here, and it is something that postgraduates worry about, particularly those who look very young. Even mature students can have their issues, but it is not your remit to persuade them to treat you as an experienced teacher.

How can you help students – at their different ages and stages – steer their way through university life? It is not your job to steer them. Help them to help themselves. This may sound irresponsible, but it is genuinely a sound way to proceed, and if you think it through, some of the alternatives do not really achieve very much, and can be very costly in terms of time. This is what lot of counsellors do: people have the potential to help themselves and their/your job is to help them break down barriers and work out solutions. This approach also chimes with current thinking about facilitating learning. There is an implicit assumption in facilitating learning – developing metacognition and so on – that students have the capacity to do this. Your role is to help them uncover meanings and develop solutions. A strength of this approach is that is it not as mechanical as some; it is based on empathy.

Key principles

- Understanding boundaries.
- Setting clear boundaries with students.
- Discussing them with students in order to make them clear.
- Making general boundaries explicit: 'This is what I can do. That is something I cannot help you with', 'What I can tell you is to go and see … who will be able to help you', 'You cannot come to see me in my office unless you email me first.'

Where are all the sources of support?

There will be a lot of information in the student handbook about support services for students at different levels in the institution. Table 7.1 lists those typical of most universities.

This is not to say that you simply refer students who bring their problems to you to the handbook; but it is an important source of up-to-date information for you. Make sure that you always have the latest version of the handbook, in case names or numbers have changed, for example.

Support in the department

Start with your department: is there a focus for these issues there? They should be the remit of some forum, a course leader or staff–student committee. Tutorials and labs tend to be contained in a department, and there is often an issue of boundary management between what is provided at department, faculty and university levels. There is often a lack of communication between these levels. You need to know what structures exist, though it is not your role to establish links between them.

For example, most universities provide a counselling service for students. This may offer one-to-one sessions. There may also be an array of other related roles, such as academic counsellors, directors of study and personal academic tutors, potentially with different titles in different institutions. Your students may not understand exactly what these roles involve either, so it might be important for you

TABLE 7.1
University support services

	DEPARTMENT	FACULTY	UNIVERSITY	STUDENT UNION
Student services			√	
Academic adviser	√			
Disability adviser	(√)	(√)	√	
Financial advice			√	√
Counselling			√	
Health advice			√	
Childcare			(√)	(√)
Learning support	(√)	(√)	√	
IT/library skills	(√)	(√)	√	
Appeals/grievances	√	√	√	√

√   Indicates service likely to be available.

(√)   Indicates service may or may not be available.

to be able to help them with that. Refer them to the person in the department, or the named person in university services, who has this role and can help. You may be the first person to hear about a student's problem, but it is unlikely that you are the best person to deal with it. Clarify this to your students and suggest other people who can help them.

All students are assigned to a personal academic tutor, normally as part of the quality assurance system. These are called different things in different universities. If you do not have one of these titles, it helps to clarify further that you cannot take responsibility for this role. However, what commonly happens is that undergraduates find that they relate to different tutors differently. It may be a personality thing. They find some tutors more approachable than others.

Support around the university

How informed are your students about what the different sources of support can offer? There is a quick way to find that out, if it is all in the class handbook: 'Let's open the handbook and turn to the page ... Let's open the web page now.' This can save you a lot of time explaining and interpreting things that are quite factual. Do not be afraid of saying, 'I really don't know much about what they do ... You are better going to their website, which is referenced in this section.'

Some universities have codes of practice on this, but others do not. Check what the regulations are concerning giving advice to students. Think through how you will use the support provided at university level. There will be a student counsellor: That would be the person to whom you refer cases that are less straightforward, not easily solved by someone in the department, perhaps the more personal issues, such as prolonged illness, family problems, psychological problems. But is this set of judgements part of your remit? It may not be up to you to decide which level of support the student should approach first. You do not have the ability to 'screen' students for the severity of their problem in the way that is implied above. Refer the student to the departmental contact.

However, there are some problems that will probably only be handled at the university level. The disabilities adviser, for example, will have expertise that will not be available in all departments. Again, however, you should first check your department: there may be a disability coordinator, who may know, for example, how the department currently handles dyslexia. At the university level, there may be a team of people. Often they can arrange – and pay for – a student to be tested for such conditions, and they can advise students and departments about any additional human and physical support that will be needed.

Once you have a clear sense of the boundaries of your remit, you may decide that you want to know more about this area. You may develop an interest in one or more of these issues and decide that you would like to develop some counselling or study skills, for example. When you contact one support service, ask them who else you should speak to. Start tapping into existing networks.

Some of this territory is usually covered in training programmes for new staff: can you get on to those? Contact staff development or educational development or the centre for teaching and learning. Even if you cannot get on their courses, you can have access to an important source of advice. This can be an important step in your development as a teacher.

There is another layer of help – the student union. There will be many different advisers for students, including financial advisers. This is a particularly important source of support for students who do not want to contact university staff. They can also help students through appeals, complaints and grievance procedures. They might also be able to help with childcare, or would have up-to-date knowledge of what help is available.

The key is providing support just-in-time. It is important that you are a port of call. A student may want to talk to someone right there, right then. A problem may have been building up for some time. Therefore, it might be appropriate for you to listen to what the student has to say, and you may want to offer confidential time. The advice to give may be straightforward. For example, if the student is worried about not finishing an assessment on time, point out that there are procedures for getting an extension and prompt the student to go, there and then, to discuss this option with the programme or course leader. In this way, you act as a kind of filter.

Even here, as you take time to listen, however, the best advice we can give you is not to get involved in counselling the student. Even if you have counselling skills, it is not your role. It is about understanding your role – and getting your students to understand it. Unless you have specifically and formally been given a role, it is not your role.

Dealing with diversity

Students may feel that they have heard all they need to know about 'diversity': equal opportunities, race relations, disabilities, cultural differences. They quickly learn that there are a lot of messages out there, but that they are not always coordinated. Check it out. Deal with it by reference. What have they heard about it? What do you need to remind them about, if anything? This saves you repeating what they have heard already. Anything that is relatively new might be worth targeting, or anything with a specific connection to your class. Otherwise, it might be more diffuse territory: 'You can tell me about diversity by email, and then we can make adjustments.'

Treat diversity of the student body as something very positive and use it in your teaching, so that students learn that there are different points of view, different perspectives. For example, use cultural differences to inform discussions in class. Set up discussions to promote this. This may be one of the best ways for you to learn about these issues: 'How does this happen in your community?'; 'How do you … tell us about …?' Be careful not to assume, or to appear to assume, that one student represents a community. In addition, be aware that the student may be biased. What they say is not to be taken as neutral. Having asked for their view, it could be complex to then have to say to someone, 'I think you're being biased', but you have to be ready to do so.

The baseline is that first of all you need to know about religious conventions: when Muslims may be fasting, and when different cultures may be celebrating holidays. This should be taken into account in the way your classes are timetabled – for example, assessment deadlines – but postgraduates cannot do much about that. Some of these things should no longer be a matter of speculation; institutions like universities should know these things and what to do about them. This is why it is so important that you know what the policy is and who your departmental contact is.

Be aware of your non-verbals, of giving the impression that you favour one student or one group. This is easier to do subconsciously than you might think.

It may be a simple matter of something you have in common – sport, culture, place – or there may be some underlying connection or attraction. You will have to manage that carefully, so as not to show it, and therefore risk accusations of bias or favouritism.

What if a student comes to you and says s/he is being harassed by another student?

HEALTH WARNING !

We suggest that you don't touch this with a bargepole.

There are others with responsibilities for issues between students.

Dealing with discrimination

In your lectures, labs and tutorials, it is your responsibility to make sure that there is no discrimination. A useful starting point is to help students to learn about what constitutes acceptable behaviour.

Ground rules for acceptable behaviour

- Respect for others: listening and valuing others' contributions.
- Taking reasonable steps to accommodate their needs.
- Being careful of one's own behaviour.
- Being alert to difficulties that students might have: for example, reorganising furniture for students in a wheelchair.
- Announcing a personal difficulty without singling out the person and without revealing your own impatience, or whatever, and finding a way to announce it. For example, if someone has a coffee allergy … perhaps not mention the allergy at all? But then people might ignore it? This may seem to be an extreme example, but it is a real one. It is your job to position this not as an extreme example, but one that the group will treat with respect. Then there are perfume allergies, nut allergies. This may be up to the individual student. They are in control of that. You are in control of how the group deals with it.

- Making sure all your learning materials are accessible.
- Obviously, watching your language: swearing and sexual references are out of order.
- Making sure your use of humour will not be offensive. For example, making sure what you see as irony is not interpreted as sarcasm.
- Not discriminating.

While no one would state that they set out to discriminate against a fellow student, we all know – surely – that it is possible to do so simply through lack of attention to students' needs, impatience with their articulation or, occasionally, defensiveness at an implied critique of you. This is, of course, avoidable.

For example, to avoid discriminating against disabled students, your starting point can be 'What do you need me to do? … Here's the extent to which I can do that … Do other people need to be brought into it? … You tell me what you need, and I'll see if I can work it out'. This is invariably seen as a positive approach. No one expects you to be an expert on every disability. Even for ones you do know about, it is still important to find out what works for the individual. Disabled people are not the same and should not be treated as if they are.

There are a number of ways for you to avoid discriminating:

- Being as inclusive as possible in the design of activities: considering various points of view and diverse cultural contexts. For example, using names from other cultures than your own, when designing case studies or scenarios. Trying to integrate different types of organisations that might be different from your own. Some case studies don't even apply to other countries.
- Defining terms and acronyms.
- Ensuring that you're not doing anything that might be seen as discriminatory in how you manage your class. For example, not ignoring students from certain groups.
- Using non-verbals carefully and learning how others use them differently.
- Applying university policy. What if a Muslim student says 'It's Ramadan. I'm not coming to class tomorrow'? If attendance is required, then you will have to advise them of that. If they object, refer them on to someone else in your department. What is the university's policy about this? This is not one you should make up as you go along. Appropriate measures will be taken, possibly by someone else, but as a tutor you should know what the policy is.

- Calling for help with cultural clashes: for example, some women from some cultures are uncomfortable working with men in groups and/or in small rooms. Some universities regard this as the students' problem; they chose to study in another culture and should adopt the norms of that culture, is the thinking. Some students will not work with students from a lower caste. You will need to take advice if, for a cultural reason, students do not want to do the task you set them.
- Helping students make a transition to a new skill/role: for example, physiotherapy students have to touch each other, and patients. If, for some reason, they do not want to do this – even though it will be central to their professional role – remember that this issue should have been addressed at an earlier stage. Someone will already have prepared the students for this activity. Your role is to act as a bridge or transition, prompting them to put what they know into practice.

For more detail on what universities – and other organisations – are required by law to do, see the references in our Introduction. This is an area where you should probably update yourself from time to time, as it affects all contexts. More importantly, you have to know the ways in which these issues have been addressed in your department. The main point for you is to acknowledge that society has had to confront discrimination and to work out how to deal with it at all levels. This is not about you trying to work out how to resolve all these problems.

Is there scope to include students in managing this area? It is as much the students' job as yours. Students, through school and work experience, should have a fair idea about gender issues and discrimination, so much so that it might be patronising to go through all of the issues with them. Wait for them to come up and remind people of what is acceptable. Things have moved on. Remind them that, in terms of hard ground rules, people accept university policies when they accept the offer of a place. It is not a question of persuading people to adopt these policies. It is no longer a matter of negotiation and goodwill; it may, instead, be matter of entitlement in some situations. However, certain specific steps may be at the discretion of the tutor or the department. If that is the case, you need to know which these are.

Dealing with difficult students – and students in difficulty

What is the difference between the 'difficult' student and the student who is 'in difficulty'? A student who identifies a difficulty in your class may express a fair amount of anxiety and may overstate the problem. Students can behave more aggressively in these situations than, perhaps, they intend. It is up to you to defuse the situation, get to the heart of the problem and tell the student what you can and cannot do to help.

If a student comes to you with a problem relating to your class, for example, about not getting on with or not being able to work with a task or lab group, you have to deal with this, because this is about teaching. Students might say, 'I feel like I'm being bullied or excluded by other members of the class' or 'I feel like I'm being discriminated against because of my race' or 'The guys in my group don't take me seriously' or 'They want me to do all the work' or 'My other tutor won't tell me what and where I'm going wrong; s/he says I have to work it out for myself.'

If the student challenges your teaching style, approach or materials, before you do anything else you need to check out the scale of the problem. Before you make any changes to your course, you need to know if others are having the same difficulties. If you have been doing regular checking, getting feedback on your teaching and student learning, then you will be well placed to put one student's comment or challenge in context. You will be able to say this to the student, while still offering to help. If, for example, the student is anxious that you are not giving your class what they need to know for the exam, you can reply: 'I'm here to facilitate your learning; I'm not here to give you the answers to the exam. I'm here to help you learn.' If there is only one student who presents with this problem, then be careful about investing too much time on this.

You have rights too. There is no need to put up with disrespect or constant challenging. The question is what to do about it, and here, again, you can learn from more experienced colleagues. The students who are being 'difficult' may just be immature, or alternatively, they may think that this is what 'critical thinking' means.

There may be students you simply do not like. It is bound to happen some time:

It is a fact of life that we don't necessarily like every person with whom we come into contact … You might find yourself feeling guilty at your negative emotions towards a particular student, but in reality you are simply being human. So long as your emotions are not apparent in the way that you treat your students … you are doing the best that you possibly can. (Cowley, 2003: 122)

Supporting students and maintaining good relationships can be complex. You need to be aware of some dos and don'ts, and some issues to refer to others.

Do's and don'ts

Don't

- Appear to criticise colleagues, come between other teaching staff and students, get emotionally involved. However, recognise that feelings are part of group contexts.
- Get out of your depth. If you feel you are out of your depth, get support, help and/or training. These are likely to be available somewhere on campus.

Do's

- Have a crisis strategy if you find yourself out of your depth. Think through what you would say. Don't just think about it all in terms of problems. Avoid 'catastrophising'. Get through it. Build confidence.

What do we mean by a crisis strategy. Examples are:

- 'I'm sorry, we'll have to stop this conversation now. I cannot respond to … What I want you to do now is … (move on to more directive mode)'.
- If a student criticises another tutor: 'I can appreciate you have difficulty here, but it would be inappropriate for me to comment. I suggest you go away and think it through and think about what you should do … and then approach that tutor.'
- Variation on 'What do you think would happen if …?' to say to students: 'What do you think would happen if you went back to the tutor and asked for clarification?'

Students often set up or envisage confrontation that is not really there, and you can help them to work through that. For example, point out that their forming a view that a tutor 'does not like them' will not get them very far.

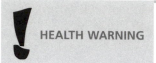

HEALTH WARNING

ISSUES THAT YOU SHOULD NOT DEAL WITH

- Medical issues – doctors and nurses, campus health service.
- Mental health – counselling or doctor as first point of contact.
- Academic issues – first port of call is academic adviser or tutor.

The last of the list in the health warning draws a distinction between issues that are to do with your own class, and formal academic processes, such as extensions and attendance.

Be realistic about what you expect first-year students, for example, to do in preparation for tutorials, if all that happens is that they get 5% or 10% of their course grade for just turning up. Besides, you will probably have a mixed group: those who are content just to pass your course and those who want to do well and continue studying in your discipline after the first year. This may explain why some of your students are consistently underprepared and others are really working hard. It might be less about your teaching and more about their motivation. It might be less a measure of their intelligence and more that they are thinking ahead to future studies, targeting their efforts elsewhere. Again, for you, it is important to clarify what the problem is without getting fixated on problems.

You can also support students who find out, perhaps late in the day, that they are on the wrong programme and want to switch or get out of university altogether. Put them in touch with academic advisers, careers service, registry, finance office and guidance services. Students should, of course, be encouraged to think before walking away or staying on, but some are not aware that they have choices, that they can walk away. Some students leave it a little late to recognise what the job opportunities following a course will be like. Careers services are very good at prompting students – and staff – to think all this through.

Whenever students bring problems or 'difficulties' to you, it is a chance for you to continue the work of constructive alignment that, as we discussed earlier, is a key process in university teaching. If students come to you with complaints that they have not had the lecture they require before your tutorial or lab, you can suggest that they do some reading, check out a website or begin to think about the subject for themselves. In this way, you are prompting them to make their own connections between all the learning activities and resources, an essential part of the learning process. Not all tutorials and labs are 'calibrated' with lectures in any case, and simply pointing this out to students would be helpful. What you do not want to find yourself doing is trying to defend the curriculum; your job is to prompt students to take responsibility for their learning. Instead of sustaining students' critique of the system, question their assumption that the course can only progress in a logical, linear or sequential way. Point out that tutorials and labs do not always follow lectures; it is not always like that. Prompt them to think about how they can make connections, whatever the order, nature or level of materials and classes they experience.

Portfolio

Practical, instrumental aspects of your teaching role will continue to provide food for thought: managing classroom furniture, audibility, handouts, audiovisuals etc.

However, you may want to move on to consider your personal experience of the role. This may be a good time to assess your level of self-confidence or self-esteem in the teaching role and to revisit your concerns about how you are perceived. You can then address the question of whether you should be managing things in a different way: 'What do you think would happen if ...?'

Asking students if they know what 'postgraduate' means, what postgraduates do and telling them why a postgraduate is taking this tutorial can put the issue out in the open, and it could be an icebreaker in your first tutorial. You can clarify by defining your role explicitly: 'My job is to make sure you have understood the lectures, and can manage your log book.' Having done this, you can now reflect on whether you think that worked well, how students responded, whether or not you would do that again.

One of the main strategies put forward in this chapter – and throughout this book – is about looking after yourself, not taking on more than you are required to or more than you are qualified to do. Where do you stand on that issue now? Have you drawn a clear line – for yourself, for your students – or are you still uncomfortable with the concept? Who can you discuss this with in your department for further insights and support?

8

Supervising Undergraduate Projects and Dissertations

I'm not technically the supervisor, but I'm more or less supervising the students.

I can't get on with my research because I'm spending so much time helping the masters students with their projects.

This chapter presents a new problem and what for many postgraduates will be a new role. In some institutions postgraduates are not allowed to supervise research. Some universities have regulations prohibiting it. Postgraduates are often effectively prevented from supervising because their institutions require new supervisors to take a course that is only offered to full-time academic staff. However, postgraduates tell us that they have been asked, perhaps 'exceptionally', to support undergraduate dissertations (and, more rarely, masters projects).

In this situation, you may not be given the title 'supervisor'. Instead, you may be asked to 'help a student out', or to give specific advice, perhaps in an episodic way, or to provide technical assistance. Then, over time, you may be asked to do this more, or for more students, and in a year or two you may find that you are, in effect, supervising research.

However it happens, you might want to be ready to take the opportunity, if it does arise, or to consider the pros and cons before you do: supervising may be good experience for you, but, as with teaching, it takes time away from your own research. Being a supervisor may even take up more of your time than teaching.

Assuming that you want to supervise, if asked, and to give you a sense of what constitutes good practice, this chapter covers the key principles of good supervision. As for all the chapters in this book, our priority is to help you make the best possible choice of approach and activity for your students.

The advice we include, while drawing on research into supervision in different disciplines, is at the basic level. For future reference, you should know that there is a growing literature on research supervision that you can consult. It is no longer necessary to model yourself on your supervisor exclusively, or to rely only on the advice of experienced supervisors in your department – although their advice can be extremely illuminating – or simply to learn by doing. All of these are important, but it is now possible to test them against policy, scholarship and research.

The key concept for this chapter is enabling your students to work independently: they have to make choices, get organised and produce a longer piece of writing, usually at a higher level, than they have before. To help them do this, you can use strategies you developed for other contexts, and covered in other chapters of this book, to get them talking, working in groups and writing. For example, your facilitation skills will be particularly relevant in supervision.

We describe specific activities you can use in supervision meetings to help students learn what doing 'research' involves. Of course, all undergraduates will have done many research activities before, but they may not see it that way. They may not see the connections. This will be one of your first tasks, to point out the relevance of such skills as literature searching to their research projects: where they see a brand new task, you can show how it builds on assessments they did in previous courses. Helping them make these connections is, arguably, as important a part of your role as your subject expertise.

Before you agree to supervise

In this section we alert you to potential problems. This is not to say that supervision is inherently problematic – though some argue that it is – but to help you prepare to solve recurring problems or, where possible, avoid them altogether.

The greatest risks for you, in taking on this role, are getting out of your depth, taking on too much and losing too much time from your own research. The person who asked you to supervise may be genuinely interested in helping you develop, but it is up to you to do some kind of risk assessment before you accept.

With all that in mind, and in the spirit of professionalism – for example, it is always your intention to do a good job – we suggest questions you can ask of whoever wants you to 'do some supervision'. You might even think of this as two sets of questions: questions you ask the person who invited you to supervise, and questions you ask elsewhere. This is not to say that you go behind his or her back; it may just be that there is 'informal intelligence', in your networks, for example, to help you make an informed decision about whether or not to take on supervision.

Questions you can ask about supervision

- Will I be working with another supervisor?
- Will I be supervising this student jointly with you ... or with someone else?
- What are the terms of that relationship?
- Who will do what?
- To your co-supervisor: have you done this before ... how does it work?
- What exactly do you see as my role?
- Which tasks would you like me to perform?
- Is there anything you think I should not do?
- Will I decide how to do these tasks, or will you guide me?
- Will you and I have time set aside to discuss our supervision?
- Does the student I will be supervising know this and know what it means?
- Will I be paid for supervising?
- If so, at what rate? A one-off payment for it all? An hourly rate?
- Is that the same rate as for teaching, or not?
- Will I be paid for each student, or will I do it all for one sum?
- Will you put all that in writing to me?

You might not want to ask all the questions at one meeting. You might be worried about overwhelming your supervisor – or whoever asked you – with what sounds like the beginnings of a negotiation, or even, to some ears, an interrogation.

There may, in fact, be a mismatch of expectations here. You are simply looking for guidance – and it may help your communications to say so explicitly a few times in this discussion – while your supervisor is looking for either (1) a way to save himself or herself time or (2) your recognition that this is an opportunity to take some initiative, and here you are slowing the whole process down by asking for guidance. You may sense their impatience, but persevere, be calm and appreciative.

In addition, there are questions you can ask about the student you would be supervising, before you make up your mind.

Finding out about the student: ask the department and/or the student

- What is the subject of the research?
- Can I have a copy of the proposal?
- Has the student done any work or preparation so far?
- Where did he or she do undergraduate work?
- When are they due to complete?
- Has the student secured ethical/other approval for the project?
- Has the student started gathering data, in any sense?
- Has this student had any problems so far with the project?
- What is the standard of written and spoken English?
- Has the student done any writing for the dissertation?

Again this will seem, to some supervisors and to some postgraduates, to be just too many questions, when what is wanted is a quick 'yes or no' from you, and preferably a 'yes': 'Yes, I will supervise this student.' It is probably worth emphasising, therefore, that you should put a little thought into how you ask these questions, for example, which words you will use. If you are still worried about how your questions will be perceived, your best strategy may be to state explicitly that you are not being suspicious or paranoid. You simply want to get to know the student. Reposition your questions as simply good professional practice, sensible preparation for supervision, particularly when you are at 'stage X' in your own research.

Think about your 'non-verbals', those sometimes involuntary signals of your intentions and reactions. You can also think about throwing in a couple of positive 'verbals': 'That's interesting … How did you/they come up with that? … Can you tell me a bit more about that? … I am interested in the aspect of … That should produce some really useful … That makes sense … I wonder if … Would that mean … How does it look so far?' Something along these lines indicates your interest in the project without committing you to taking it on – although, again, you might want to make this explicit, in case your apparent interest is taken as tacit acceptance of the role.

You can always ask the student some of these questions, but it is interesting to hear the department's answers. Do not feel that you can only ask questions once;

it can be quite revealing, in a positive way, to ask questions of the department or supervisor about the student, and of the student himself or herself. Of course, you do not have to tell the student that you are still making up your mind about whether or not to take on their supervision – although you might think it fairer to do so, some students will feel it puts them under pressure – but you can play the role of a fellow researcher who is interested in the research.

If this all seems too covert or paranoid, think through the scenario of having a problem student passed to you, when you were not aware (1) that the student had a serious problem of some kind and (2) that the problem was so serious that the student was unlikely to complete, no matter how good your supervision was. It has happened. The supervisor who passes a student on to another supervisor may genuinely believe that the solution lies in a fresh approach, a new voice, with your relative inexperience cast as a potential advantage. The decision about whether or not to supervise a particular student lies, of course, with you; but this is why we advise you to find out about the student first, if you can.

While no one will openly admit that there is such a thing as a 'problem' student – not once a student has been admitted, and therefore judged to have the ability to complete the programme – you can find out more than you might expect from informal discussions with others in the department. Some academics will find this offensive: their position is that students are not admitted to a university unless they have the required capacity and qualifications. However, others will admit that in the real world it is not always as simple as that: students with the required qualifications do have problems, problems that are beyond your ability to influence at this stage, or problems that may simply take up too much of your time. Your priority is to finish your research. On the other hand, you may find that you are able to turn a problem case around, that you learn a lot from that, and that your standing in the department is enhanced as a result. It is difficult to predict how this will go.

If there is time, discuss the supervisor's role in your discipline, at the undergraduate (or masters) level. You can learn a lot from 'tame experts' who are prepared to share their knowledge.

Ask the experts

- What is dissertation supervision all about?
- How is it similar to and different from doctoral supervision?
- Are there recurring problems I should know about?
- What are the best ways of resolving them?

- Are there warning signs I should look out for?
- How do you know when you're doing a good job?
- How do you know when you're not?
- What do you do when … [anticipate problems you/student might have]?

In addition, scope out what exactly would be required of you as a supervisor from talking to other postgraduates who have supervised. What was it like for them? Did they have any support? Were there any problems? Did they enjoy it? What did they get out of it? Did it affect their research in any way? Did it hold it up at all?

At the very least, such discussion, along with your reading of this chapter, will give you a broader sense of how to play the role than you get from simply observing your own supervisor, brilliant though he or she may be at the role. This is the key: even if you have no time to read up on supervision, you can learn a lot from these discussions. This is, after all, a learning experience for you: to a certain extent you do learn as you go, but you can also learn in the usual array of ways, through reading, mentoring, websites and courses.

Learning about supervision

- Talk to experienced supervisors, for example, to more than one.
- Do a literature search on research supervision.
- Look at literature in other disciplines (there may be nothing in yours).
- Read a couple of books or chapters.
- Read a couple of papers, preferably research based.
- Select a couple of websites on supervision.
- Attend a course.
- Set up peer observation of your practice.

If there is a course on research supervision at your institution, ask if you can attend 'exceptionally', particularly if you were asked to supervise 'exceptionally'. Even if the course is intended for staff, persuade the director of staff development, and/or the course tutor, to make an exception. Since course participants usually include members of academic staff who are doing doctorates, you will be at a similar level to them in terms of research experience.

What is your role?

There are many ways of defining the supervisor's role. In fact, it has been argued that those who do it well play several different, sometimes contradictory, roles. However, as a new supervisor you may prefer to simplify. Your department may, in any case, only use one of the available terms:

- supervisor;
- co-supervisor;
- second supervisor;
- mentor;
- tutor;
- director;
- adviser;
- postgraduate 'helper';
- technical 'support'.

There is not much point in us defining what we mean by each of these terms, since each of them has many potential meanings. You have to find out not only which term is used for your role – and to use it in all your future discussions with students and colleagues – but also what the term means locally, in your department.

- Is your job title written down somewhere?
- In a university document? Do you have a copy?
- Do students have it? Have they read it? Do they understand it?

In practice, students may not have read the document that defines your role, and you yourself may find it difficult to make sense of it. It can be difficult working out what such documents should mean in practice. Some supervisors find it difficult even to track down a copy of the relevant document. All the more reason for you and your students to use it as an agenda – rather than a contract – for your initial discussions. This is when you make it clear and explicit what your role is – and what it is not – to the person who will be most affected by your performance, your student.

A variation in the supervisor's role is giving another postgraduate some 'technical support' or 'tuition'. For example, you may have reached a point where you are more expert in certain aspects of methodology than your supervisor is, and hence it makes sense to ask you to 'teach' this to other postgraduates (or even masters students). Of course, none of these options constitutes full-blown 'supervision', but it can happen that, as you take on one role – tuition – other tasks are added until you are, in effect, supervising research.

What exactly does supervision involve?

- How much time should you spend with your students?
- How much time are you supposed/required to give them?
- Is there a minimum/maximum number of hours?
- How many meetings must you have per term/semester during their projects?
- Are you responsible for giving feedback on drafts?
- On drafts of all sections of the dissertation or just some of them?
- Will you have to mark the dissertations you supervise, or not?
- What records will you have to keep?
- How should they be kept? In what form?
- What do you do with them?

While these questions are difficult to answer for doctoral supervision, there are often quite specific guidelines for undergraduate dissertations. You need to check.

Whatever your local guidelines say about your role, it is your job to establish (1) who you are working with, (2) what they need from you and (3) whether or not you can provide that for them. Do some early diagnostic work with them to establish who you are dealing with. You may see this as beyond your remit; it is not up to you to assess them. Or is it? You do not have to call it a 'diagnostic test'. You might, instead, ask the student to do a bit of writing, or a short presentation to get an insight into the standard of their written and spoken communication, their thinking about the subject and their understanding of what constitutes research. The purpose is to bring potential problems to the surface. At the same time, you want your students to perceive what is and is not a problem, and you want them to feel comfortable bringing their research problems to you, if that is your remit. This is part of their learning process; you can give them feedback on their work.

This may indeed feel like travelling beyond your remit, but if you delay in getting a sense of whether or not a student you are supervising can complete brief writing, speaking or reporting tasks, you might have more complex and time-consuming problems waiting for you down the line.

When you see how a student performs a task you may form the view that he or she is working at too basic a level. This is when you have to remind yourself – and possibly regularly thereafter – that the student is working at the undergraduate (or masters) level. It is not a doctorate; the purpose of the project is for them to learn about doing small-scale research, probably for the first time.

If you are not sure what is an appropriate standard of work, check with someone in your department. Do not persist with this particular uncertainty. More importantly, acknowledge that you are still learning about what represents an acceptable and appropriate standard of work. You are not going to learn very much about that from supervising one student or even, perhaps, from the first time you supervise or co-supervise several students. You need to get a second opinion from time to time. That is the sensible and professional thing to do. If you feel like you are going too often to experienced supervisors for advice, vary your approach by, for example, sounding them out about your emerging views. Most supervisors will usually set you right, if you are wrong, or offer their views, if they differ or agree. If they do not offer views, ask.

From your students' perspective, it may not matter how you define your role. They will be much more interested in what you can offer in terms of time, number of meetings and availability for them. Set limits from the start.

What your dissertation students need to know

- How many meetings will you have with them over the project's lifecycle?
- How long will each meeting be?
- Can they contact you between meetings?
- By email? Or?
- Are you generally available to them or only at fixed times?

If your department stipulates a limit to the number of hours you do, there must, by definition, be a limit to the extent to which you can troubleshoot for problems in students' projects. There will then be a limit to what you can do to help students solve their problems, and, consequently, a limit to your responsibility for anything that goes wrong. In theory. Again, not everyone will see it that way all of the time. Expectations differ. All the more reason to get them out in the open at the start. If no one else appears to be doing so, it is up to you to take the initiative.

What is 'research' at undergraduate level?

Your role is to help students answer this question and to help them make connections with their earlier work and assessments. This should be straightforward, since you have been doing research for some time now, but the challenge for you is to scale down the scope of projects for the undergraduate level. More importantly, you have to get your students to do so, to get them to form a clear idea of what is 'enough' for a project, what is 'too much' and what is actually feasible in the months – rather than years – that they have to do it in. This is an essential step, and you must make time for students to understand this point.

Getting students to think and talk about research

- Talk about your experience of designing research projects.
- What was doing your undergraduate project like?
- Demonstrate the thinking and writing tasks involved.
- Help them see it as a process.
- If they have to write proposals, go through the structure.
- Prompt them to rehearse their proposals in discussion.

As for any other form of assessment, there will be criteria. What are they and what do they mean? Some of them will be familiar to students, but they will probably want to know whether any of the terms they recognise mean something different at this level.

In some institutions, in some subjects, more marks are awarded to certain sections of the completed dissertation, such as the literature review and discussion, for example. In your department this may apply too, but perhaps not in exactly the same way. Or it may not apply at all. Find out and go through it with students:

if there are more marks allocated, what does that mean in terms of length, content, level of detail, etc., that they need to produce in their chapters?

If you are to be the dissertation marker, you might want to find a mentor to advise you. There may be a system of blind double-marking in your department, but you can do some practice marking first.

Finally, do not feel that you have to be an expert in every subject that the students are researching. What you do have is experience of research design and procedures, and that is what they need to learn about.

Helping students to manage the research process

You can help your students plan the lifecycle of their projects, using planning templates such as those at http://www.strath.ac.uk/Departments/CAP/dissertation/. You can use these templates in different ways:

- Use the templates to illustrate the kind of thing students can do to plan their projects. This lets you check that they are being realistic, not taking on too much, planning something that is feasible. You can check that they are making time for regular writing, and not leaving it all till the end, as some are tempted to do.
- Using the templates, devise, or have the student(s) devise, an initial research task – for example, to produce timetables for the whole project.
- You can use the templates to monitor students' completion of tasks, letting you – and them – see where their research process is progressing, where it breaks down, and giving you opportunities to provide support and corrective advice, as required.
- Or just point them in the direction of the website, giving them the reference, although experience suggests that they will not use it in the above ways unless you build this into your supervision practice and, by doing so, into their research practice.

Even if you only use the templates as a starting point, they prompt students to make decisions about time allocation over the long term, for the whole project, and to set goals for the short term, for each week or month. Prompt your students to create milestones in their projects, helping you to help them monitor their progress.

In the first stage, there are key tasks in every research project that you can help your students to initiate, as shown below. You may, of course, identify other key tasks, or they may be identified for you, if your department operates a structured approach to research projects. Each of these can then be the focus of a meeting with your student(s). Alternatively, if you are allocated only one meeting, you may have to get through all of these in one hour.

Key research tasks

- Developing a research question or hypothesis.
- Narrowing down the terms of the question.
- Designing the project.
- Securing ethical approval.
- Establishing what resources they will need.

The first meeting: supervising your students in a group

One of the best ways of getting students to learn about what constitutes research is to work through examples of completed dissertations with them, an activity that you can use with groups of students. (Frequently, in undergraduate projects, supervisors have more than one student.)

The advantage of seeing all your students together is that it saves you time. If you have five students, have a one-hour introductory meeting, rather than five hours covering more or less the same ground with each of them. For students, there are potential learning outcomes.

Advantages of seeing your students in a group

- You discover their misconceptions about 'research' and correct them.
- You prompt them to develop connections with their earlier assignments.
- It establishes subgroups and 'buddy' relationships.
- Meetings build a group effect.
- Discussions expose a range of research questions.

- Discussions reveal a range of possible strategies.
- Students rehearse their plans, ideas and arguments in a safe forum.
- Action planning occurs in an open forum.
- Supervisors can help students make realistic plans.

Organise the group discussion so that your students can formulate their own questions, rather than listening to you talk for an hour and then wondering if their questions are appropriate or too simplistic and basic. (See Chapter 3 for suggestions on managing group discussions.) Open discussion can develop their confidence in asking questions. They begin to see that they have choices to make about how they carry out their research.

The full process of organising the initial discussion with a group of students is described by Thow and Murray (2001) in a paper that includes a template structure for dissertations, a supervisor's first-hand account of the meeting and students' frequently asked questions.

The structure of this meeting can be dictated by the structure of dissertations in your department. Work through the chapters of completed dissertations, getting students to voice their understanding of the purpose of each chapter and to give a view on how the research was conducted and written up.

One of the most helpful strategies appears to be to prompt students to visualise the whole dissertation, by drawing a graphical display, and then asking them to consider word allocations for each chapter and the associated considerations of level of detail, complexity, proportion, logic and coherence of the overall argument or report. Students report that while the total word length of a dissertation is daunting, this approach makes the writing task seem manageable. More importantly, as they analyse completed dissertations in this discussion, they will see that there is more than one way of designing a dissertation.

In this discussion, rather than trying to teach them 'all they need to know' about doing a research project and writing a dissertation, prompt them to think about what that might involve for them, for different types of project. Instead of trying to anticipate all their questions, prompt them to voice the questions that occur to them, as they occur to them, and deal with them in that sequence. This can mean that the learning is paced better and is more suited to the students' needs: they find out what they need to know as they need to know it. They engage with problems posed by research and dissertation writing, not just in general terms, but in terms of their own emerging research projects.

What questions do students ask? One question that particularly bothers them, before they even start, and that might therefore cause them to get bogged down at an early stage, is, 'What does critiquing the literature mean … how do you do that?' This may be the first time they have been asked to do that – although you might think that it is a task implicit in many of their previous assignments – and it raises the question of authority. Who are they to critique authorities in their field, people with much more experience than they have, people who know much more about the subject?

Explain briefly what the term 'critiquing' means: for example, you might say that critiquing means identifying what research has and has not achieved, perhaps by design. Refer to the completed dissertations you are using in this discussion for ways of putting this into words. This is a crucial step, since the students then see, in words and paragraphs, what exactly they have to do. More importantly, they see that there is more than one way of doing it.

It is important that they spend some time observing – for example, skimming, scanning and reading – how the structure of a dissertation is signalled. It is probably more useful to do this during your meeting than to tell them to do it on their own, by the next meeting.

A key benefit of such discussions is that you find out what misconceptions students have. For example, they frequently think that they must finish their literature reviews before they do anything else. Rather than telling them in advance all the dos and don'ts, let them express their thoughts and expectations and take time, and discussion, to think them through. Correcting misconceptions, without stopping students talking or thinking for themselves, draws as much on your facilitation skills as on your research experience (see Chapter 3).

What to say to students in subsequent meetings

Time for supervision meetings may be short at this level. You may have a limited number of meetings and limited time for each. It is crucial, therefore, that you establish priorities for meetings. While the first meeting was pretty 'free-flowing', subsequent meetings have to be more structured. In fact, you can develop a routine for monitoring progress, using recurring questions. These are not intended to develop a checklist mentality either for you or for your students; instead, they are prompts for discussion.

For example, three key questions are useful recurring questions. They help you get a sense of what your students are doing, how they are developing their projects, what difficulties they are having and how effective they are at problem-solving. More importantly, they help you to focus on each project because, with the best will in the world, since the previous meeting you may have lost track of what each project is about.

What have you been doing since our previous meeting?   This not only brings you up to speed with where the project is at; it also refreshes your memory on what the project is all about. It is also a useful rehearsal for students. Ask them to stop from time to time in their narratives and suggest that they write some things down, if they have not already done so. For example, if they are actively rehearsing aspects of their methods, they will verbalise steps they have taken, their reasons for doing so and things they decided not to do. All of that is potential material for their dissertations. If you ask them to write something down during your supervisions, you are helping them to integrate writing in their research. This is not to say that what they write then is what they will finally include in the dissertation, nor will they use all the points discussed. In fact, you can discuss this point with them. Help them do what might be seen as pre-rough draft writing, sketching and listing, or 'sentencing' of points to be developed later.

Have you had any problems?   This opens the door for students to reveal difficulties with the research. Ask a follow-up question: 'What have you tried to solve that problem?'. Give credit for steps taken and make further suggestions, as appropriate. If you do make suggestions, you can deliberately make several, rather than privileging one, in order to prompt the student to think them through: what are the pros and cons of each? If, on the other hand, you have a student who never has any problems, you should still check what work has been done.

What writing have you done?   This question may throw them initially. They may not be sure, in the course of the project, what exactly they can be writing. (There are suggestions under the first question above.) If so, reinforce points you may have made earlier about dissertation structure: the contents, the template, their version of it for their projects. Simply sketching a structure for their dissertations counts as 'writing' in the early stages.

Use these questions in all your meetings; there is no compulsion to find new questions for each meeting. You will, of course, develop your own repertoire, and there will be questions you want to ask that are specific to the projects, but these questions will serve as a start.

Discuss this practice with your students. Reveal the supervision strategies you are using, name them, give your rationale for them and get students talking about what they think about your practice. If a student feels that your use of recurring questions makes meetings too predictable, point out how useful it is for you to hear what each student has been doing, thinking and writing in his or her own words. Point out that their answers to the three questions are not the same every time. Remind them of your responsibility to monitor their progress. Of course, your students will have other topics to put on the agenda, but you may find that you can get their issues covered in the course of asking these three questions.

A student may suggest that it is only your lack of experience that limits you – and them – to these questions. You can comfortably say that, yes, you do have limited experience of supervision, but you can reassure them that (1) your experience was judged sufficient for the task (possibly explaining how it is), (2) these key questions are drawn from the supervision literature, and (3) the questions do work to help you and the student explore the key topics of progress and problems. For supervision, you can tell your students, this is the bottom line: you must have a way of getting them to talk about what they are doing and to get them to open up about problems. It helps, in this conversation, if you can be reassuring rather than defensive, perhaps using some of the terms we use in this paragraph. In fact, you might not wait until you are challenged to discuss this.

What if you cannot 'solve' all their problems? It is unlikely that you will be able to fix everything. Ask someone with more experience and knowledge for support and guidance. Your role is less to be the all-round researcher and more to be listening, prompting and stimulating your students to debate, question and formulate their ideas.

Finally, there is what is arguably your most important task: whether or not your department requires it, make sure there is a written record of your supervision meetings. Get your students to prepare agendas and to make a note of each meeting. Ask them to email you a copy. This recording process serves three important purposes:

1   for students, prompting them to take an active role in managing their projects;
2   for departments, creating a 'history' and evidence that supervision took place;
3   for you, evidencing good practice and development.

The information you – or your students – record need not be lengthy. It can be a very brief note. What will you call it: a note of the meeting, or minutes? Or will you develop a monitoring form? Perhaps your department has one you can use? Perhaps there is one for doctoral supervision, but not for undergraduate projects? Can you adapt it? Do you need permission to do so? If so, from whom?

Dissertation supervision meetings
Monitoring form

Student's name: ....   *Supervisor's name:* ....

- Date of meeting.
- Topics discussed.
- Progress since last meeting.
- Agreed goals/objectives.
- Actions for student and supervisor.
- Date of next meeting.

While you have to take into account legal requirements on the use of student information, you can use notes of meetings to reflect on your growing understanding and developing practice as a supervisor.

By doing this, you are not just providing material for quality assurance purposes – important though that is. You are also tutoring your students in project management: using agendas to focus and structure meetings, recording decisions and setting goals to be achieved by the next meeting. There are, therefore, benefits to managing undergraduate supervision meetings semi-formally: benefits for students, for your department/institution and for yourself.

Getting your students to write as they go

As a junior supervisor you may not feel that you can take this on, but, in fact, there are some useful things you can do. Besides, if you do not get your students writing at an early stage, you let them run the risk of not completing on time.

Many students – and many supervisors – assert that writing is what you do after you have completed the research. However, that need not be true for all students or for all projects. In fact, you know from your own experience how important writing is for developing – not just documenting – knowledge and understanding.

Consequently, it may be important to guide your students on what exactly 'write as you go' means in the context of a small-scale research project. Most students recognise that a dissertation is not something they can write the night before the deadline, but few of them know what to do instead.

Teaching students about dissertation writing

- Discuss what the criteria mean and how they can meet them in their writing.
- Identify writing milestones throughout the project, from start to finish.
- Describe writing stages: outlining, sketching, composing, revising.
- Give them time to do each of these during your meetings.

This is a tricky one, since many students do not know what they do not know and are unlikely to ask for support at the right time. Instead, they will certainly beat a path to your door for help with their writing as the deadline approaches.

Talk about writing as an integral part of the research process: identify the writing tasks appropriate for each stage. Even if you have only been asked to help a student with some technical aspect of their project, prompt them to write it up there and then. This way, at this time, they can note the reasons for the choice of one methodology, and rejection of others, as they make those decisions. More importantly, prompt them to rehearse what they will actually write. Offer suggestions about where, in a dissertation, such writing could go, and which words should be used, thus introducing the conventions of academic writing in your discipline at this level.

This is to say not that you have to become a 'writing teacher', but that discussing writing is a crucial part of your role. Getting students to do some writing when they are with you is not as ridiculous as it sounds. It gets them to document their work and develop their thinking. If you prompt them, they can even do so in the appropriate language and style. As they do this, you can identify where their thinking is still developing – and so can they. You can give them feedback immediately.

Consider the implications of not discussing writing with students. Writing is then, literally, absent from the research process; your students will not learn exactly how writing at this level differs, if at all, from other writing they have done; and, worst of all, they may not know exactly how to write about research. They will have so many questions about writing and may, in fact, not be sure how to ask questions about writing, without sounding as if they need remedial help, which is how such questions are often treated. They often pick up the signal that they should 'just get on with it', that 'it's the quality of the research that matters, not the writing' and that reading a couple of completed dissertations will 'tell you all you need to know'. It is no wonder, when you think about it, that so many projects are not completed on time.

Specific generic prompts for writing are provided in the 'writing space' in the dissertation writing website http://www.strath.ac.uk/Departments/CAP/dissertation/. Generic prompts (see box) are those that are in use, in different forms, in many different disciplines. If some of these do not seem to fit your discipline, adapt them.

Generic prompts for dissertation writing

- The aim of the study was …
- The approach used was … I used the X approach to …
- The literature shows that …
- The hypothesis was …
- The research questions/aims/objectives were …

There are, of course, other types of prompts, or other styles of writing, that you might think suit your discipline better. It might be helpful to tell your students what they are. They are all going to have to write something along these lines. You could help your students by giving them prompts for writing such essential elements of their dissertations.

Getting your students to complete the dissertation on time

This is probably the single most serious problem in dissertation supervision, particularly if your students are part-time or off-campus or both. Many masters students, for example, are in full-time jobs. This can be excellent, if, for example, their research is related to their workplace and has, for them and perhaps for their employers, real-world relevance. However, there is also a downside: they find it more difficult to protect time for their research and to structure their time towards their deadline than do full-time students.

You might feel students' late completions would be the single most visible sign of your failure. Of course, it is not your fault; numerous factors affect their ability to complete a research project, and you are unlikely to know them all, for any one student at any given time, let alone to help them deal with them all. Yet, is it not your responsibility to ensure that they submit on time?

What can you do to help students complete on time? Simply referring them to the website with its templates is unlikely to make much difference. 'Giving structure' is crucial, but getting students to create it for themselves is what will work. Undergraduate project peer groups can help, but it might be up to you to set them up.

Perhaps the most important strategy is to embed the planning templates discussed above – or any other structuring tool – in your supervision. There is evidence that such templates, when integrated by the course tutor or supervisor, help students to complete their research on time (Strachan et al., 2004). You might want to share this finding with your students, to help them see the purpose of such tools.

Finally, sooner or later you will find that some students will not be able to finish on time. At some stage you will come across some who have serious personal problems, ranging from visas to viruses. Find out what support services your university has for counselling, financial advice and spiritual support, for example (see Chapter 7). The international office may help overseas students with a range of problems. Above all, document what you did to help.

Getting your own research finished on time

It may be an obvious point, but remember that sometimes – some will argue always – you have to put yourself first. Your priority is to finish your doctorate.

Ask yourself the question, 'Is this the right time for me to be taking on supervision?' Yes, you may learn a lot, and it may boost your confidence. Yes, it may raise your status in the department and your standing with your supervisor. Or it may not.

Take stock. What else have you got to do at this stage in your research? If you have your first conference presentation coming up, a paper to revise for a journal, and visits or experiments to collect data, then you may feel that now is not the time. Perhaps later. Alternatively, you may thrive on exactly this type of combination of challenges. It certainly prepares you for balancing tasks in the 'real world' of work in academic and other contexts.

Without going into full-blown crisis mode, if you decide not to supervise, explain your decision as the result of a rational, even analytical process. You have given it careful thought. You have weighed the pros and cons, and so on.

Remember also there are people out there who do go about actively undermining others. This may not happen to you, but it is as well to see it as a possibility and to recognise it when it happens. Some people are always putting spokes in other people's wheels, for whatever reason. Think through what is important to you and watch out for that feeling that you have to do everything you are asked to do. When you find yourself thinking that, stop to think it through. Remind yourself that it is in everyone's interest that you finish on time.

Portfolio

Throughout this chapter we have indicated ways in which you can document your experience as a supervisor. Here are four ways of using your initial experience of supervision to further your understanding and/or to evidence your development:

1   Like teaching, supervision experience can be 'good for the CV', but what have you learned? Was it what you expected? How did it compare with what you were told? Who did you talk to? What did they advise? Was any advice contradictory? Or confusing? Or particularly helpful?

2   If you followed up on further reading, you can document that:

   (a)   What did you learn from reading this chapter?

   (b)   How did it compare with what you read elsewhere?

   (c)   How did it compare with what you heard from other supervisors/students?

   (d)   Did you look at and use the planning templates website?

   (e)   Did you read the 'supervising in groups' paper?

   Have these affected your practice in any way? How did your students react?

3   What exactly did you do? You will have some record of discussions where, for example, you 'unpacked' your approach to supervision with your student(s). How did that go? How did the student(s) react?

4   In the course of learning to do supervision, you may have learned some things about yourself. Has it changed how you see your own supervisor? Has it affected how you see the process of your own research? What do you still have to learn?

Finally, can you synthesise all that: in the course of supervising one or more students, have you altered or consolidated your initial definition of good practice?

9

Programme Validation and Module Management: Quality Assurance and All That

I didn't think this was something I would be interested in but, having had a brief overview, I now understand much more about these 'events' that seem to be so important to staff. Wow, what a lot of work.

Why do you need to read this chapter?

In this chapter we deal with the bigger – and possibly more political – dimension of higher education institutions which relates to quality of provision. What do we mean by 'quality' in education? If you said that it means high standards of teaching, good facilities and other resources for learning, curricula that are fit for purpose and informed by research, developments and innovation, robust systems for student support, and equality and fairness in all interactions with students, you would be right. 'Quality' is a concept we all share and understand fairly well, but what may not be so well understood is how we achieve it, measure it, maintain it and improve it, and why it might be worthwhile to do so.

In discussing these topics, we first address the question, from a wider perspective, of why we need to think about quality. After contextual definitions and terms of reference, we explain how universities establish and maintain quality and how it is monitored.

Postgraduates often tell us that these are processes they do not know much about. Some of your colleagues might even say, 'You don't need to know this.' The point, however, is that quality in education is the responsibility of everyone – and that includes you in your role as facilitator of learning. If you do not understand the big picture, it will be more difficult for you to know where you fit into it, even though your role may be limited. Lastly, therefore, we discuss your responsibilities and where your role fits into the local (departmental) arena and into territory beyond that. It is important not to dismiss these processes as bureaucratic 'busy work', even if you hear others making such comments. Finding out what you need to know both locally and more widely is part of taking a professional approach and attending to your development towards an academic position.

Before we go on, it is worth establishing some definitions of terms which will vary in institutions. For simplicity we will adhere to these definitions and ask readers to translate to their own institutional structures. A programme is a full course of study leading to an award such as BSc or MBA (these are sometimes called courses). Programmes are often composed of components, called modules, for which students receive credit. Students must pass a determined number of modules to accumulate credits that contribute to their final award.

Why is quality in learning and teaching important?

The big picture

The first and foremost answer to this question is: because our students surely should have the best quality learning experiences we can provide. As professional academics we should continually aspire to be better designers and facilitators of that learning, and to campaign for the best resources we can. That will not be easy in a climate of constant change and budget constraints, but it is important to keep the focus on students. A number of different stakeholders are interested in assessing and monitoring the quality of learning and teaching in universities and colleges. After all, they have an investment – financial, political, social and/or personal. Some of these stakeholders are government agencies, such as the funding councils, who distribute institutional teaching budgets, and, in the UK, the Quality Assurance Agency (QAA), which is responsible for monitoring quality. Other stakeholders with a direct involvement in quality are professional bodies, students and employers. Still other stakeholders may not be directly involved but will have an interest in quality of teaching as parents, family members and taxpayers.

So quality is a high profile dimension of university business. All stakeholders want to be convinced they are getting the best value education for the money, and that students will be well prepared for their careers. The agencies of government, especially, need to convince the public that their taxes are being used effectively and efficiently. Students, who increasingly view themselves as 'customers', want to be convinced they are getting a high quality education for their fees. Professional bodies are concerned that the quality of education students receive will ensure that graduates are competent, capable and confident new practitioners in their field.

However, there are other issues at global, national and local levels; these mainly relate to reputation and recruitment. You have only to listen to the news or read the papers to be aware of university league tables, which are published each year and rank universities according to the quality of their teaching and research. Although the scores can be variously constructed and interpreted, no university wants to be at the bottom of the league tables. Furthermore, university principals take them seriously, primarily because they can be damaging to the institution's profile. If the university does well, however, it will use its rankings at every opportunity to enhance its reputation. Why? Because students mean money. In an environment in which public funding for higher education is continually shrinking and government policy is to widen access, recruitment of students is fiercely competitive. In a world where education has 'gone global', reputation is critical to marketing and student recruitment.

The institutional dimension

However, quality is not only about justifying your work to stakeholders. Nothing stands still in higher education, and institutions have to respond to external and internal change. Quality processes provide excellent opportunities for institutions to check what works and what does not and to modify and refine their systems and curricula. In the UK there have been several national agendas which universities have been required to address – widening access, student diversity, learning and teaching strategies, transferable skills and information technology. The application of quality processes, which we briefly outline below, helps the organisation to identify where it stands, what changes should occur, how they might be implemented, how they will be monitored and who will be responsible. We should also remember that quality processes are important because they identify excellence and innovation where they might otherwise lie buried and not be shared.

One further point to make here is that quality processes themselves are subject to change, so that, in fact, it sometimes seems that everything is continuously moving. Nothing stands still in higher education.

By now, you may be wondering what we mean by 'quality processes'.

What, exactly, do we mean by 'quality'?

Quality is a term which refers to all the opportunities for learning which help students to attain their award. In this context 'learning opportunities' includes everything that supports learning, such as the curriculum, teaching, academic pastoral support, assessment and feedback, student services, library, IT and laboratory facilities. Other terms associated with quality that you should know about are given in the box. The discussion which follows will elaborate on all of these, except quality audit, which you are unlikely to have anything to do with.

Quality: in academic contexts, quality is defined by how well the learning opportunities that are available to students support them to achieve their award.

Quality assurance: quality assurance is a term which encompasses the processes within an institution which guarantee and monitor quality.

Quality audit: quality audit is the process whereby expenditure is tracked and documented. Is the public's money being well spent?

Quality enhancement: quality enhancement refers to the deliberate steps taken to improve the learning experiences of students based on evaluation, implementation and dissemination.

How do we manage quality?

Internal systems

All universities in the UK have strict quality assurance systems which:

- Subject all new programmes to stringent peer scrutiny prior to granting permission for the programme to recruit students. This is called *validation*.
- Review all existing programmes, normally on a three- or five-year cycle, through the same peer scrutiny, prior to granting further permission for the programme to continue. This is called *triannual or quinquennial review*.
- Review all existing programmes every year, through written reports, in order to identify and address any difficulties arising throughout the term of validation. This is usually called *annual monitoring or annual review*.
- Review and approve (or reject) the addition or withdrawal of modules and changes to modules to ensure that the integrity of programmes is not affected by proposed changes. This is particularly important if modules are shared by several programmes, for instance 'study skills' or 'introduction to research methods'.
- Review provision in addition to the programme-based systems described above. This may take the form of thematic reviews. For example, the

university quality committee may decide to review assessment and feedback to students, or collaborative programmes, or employability in the curriculum. In large institutions departments may be reviewed on a rotating or sampling basis, and the review would take the form of questionnaires, interviews and document analysis.

Perhaps these systems help to explain why it is not possible to just invent a course or module and run it tomorrow. It is the responsibility of staff to put forward a strong and robustly justified case for introducing new programmes and modules. This is not only because of the need for quality assurance, but also because courses are expensive propositions, and the institution will not enter into a new venture lightly.

Because validation, review and annual monitoring are the most common forms of quality assurance, and are those most likely to touch postgraduates, we focus on these.

Validation

All programmes in all universities must be validated before they can become operational and recruit students. The purpose of validations is to ensure that programmes meet the needs of all their stakeholders, that they meet the criteria and benchmarks for standards and quality, and that sufficient resources have been committed for them to run. Generally, programmes are validated for five or three years, after which they must be 'reviewed' (see below).

Step 1: programme outline or statement of intent   The programme team submits an outline for the proposed programme, based on market research, competition, forecasting, resources (staffing, library, IT, facilities), staff development, specialist equipment, materials, etc. Agreement that planning can proceed will be based on the capacity of the institution to finance and support it. It must also fit the strategic development of the university's academic portfolio, that is, the profile of programmes and courses it offers.

Step 2: programme development   The programme team in the department, or in collaboration with other departments, designs the programme in consideration of:

- potential student market;
- aims and learning outcomes;
- structure, content and mode of delivery;
- university regulations and support infrastructure;

- demands from external bodies, for example, professional bodies such as the British Psychological Society or the General Medical Council;
- government agendas, for example, widening access, disabilities and equal opportunities legislation;
- university strategic priorities, for example, curriculum investment, web-based learning, collaborative partnerships.

The design includes assessments, learning and teaching approaches, placement learning (if relevant), quality assurance arrangements, entry requirements, student support mechanisms, all the modules with their descriptors. The programme team may include external members representing professions or employers and students to help them respond to the needs of these stakeholders. This process may take up to a year, involving numerous meetings of the team and its subgroups, lots of thinking and writing, and plenty of paperwork.

A validation document, which describes and defends the purpose and character of the programme, is the main outcome of all the work. Other accompanying documents include the collected curricula vitae (CVs) of the teaching team, to verify that the staff are properly qualified to deliver the programme; a student handbook, demonstrating what information will be given to students on the programme; and, if appropriate, a placement and/or dissertation handbook.

Step 3: validation   The validation event is organised by administrative staff normally residing in the registry. They usually have overall responsibility for quality procedures; this also includes university governance and regulations, admissions, student records, assessments and awards. All the validation documents will be distributed to members of a validation panel for scrutiny prior to the validation event. The validation panel will include internal staff from other departments and externals who represent stakeholders, such as employers or professional bodies. At the validation event, the panel will meet with the programme team. The panel will question; the team will defend and justify their programme. This is all done in the spirit of professional debate. The role of the validation panel is to confirm, by 'validating' the programme, that it is of sufficient quality to run and can recruit students.

Validation events are not intended to be combative, but should be constructively challenging. Questioning needs to be rigorous, and the ethos of the event is about stimulating debate which is meant to be thorough, not intimidating or threatening. The panel will scrutinise every element of the programme through the documentation, but it will decide in a pre-meeting what areas it wishes to probe, so that questions can be quite focused.

Sample validation questions

- Could you explain the underpinning philosophy of this programme?
- What is the key conceptual framework which informs the delivery of this programme?
- Where, within the programme, do you develop students' work-related transferable skills, and how are those assessed?
- What arrangements have you made to support direct entrants from further education?
- What role have employers had in the development of your programme, and where would we see their influence on the curriculum?
- How will you ensure that quality assurance arrangements will be implemented by your overseas partners?

The panel will also ask questions of senior staff to assure themselves that the programme will be satisfactorily resourced in terms of staff and facilities. All the scrutiny and questioning done by the panel is to convince themselves that:

- The design is fit for purpose, coherent and well grounded in theory and educational research.
- The programme meets the needs of potential students and other stakeholders.
- Quality assurance arrangements are adequate to ensure the quality of the programme for the duration of the validation.
- Staffing and resources (books, IT, labs, etc.) are sufficient to enable students to study in a satisfactory environment.
- Learning, teaching and assessment are appropriate, aligned and innovative.
- Student academic support will be robust.
- There will be satisfactory support for students with disabilities.
- Entry requirements, progression regulations and placement arrangements are satisfactory.
- The programme responds to external demands and drivers.

The panel arrives at a decision about whether the programme can run or not; this takes the form of a 'validation' which is granted, normally, for either three or five years. Often the panel sets conditions which must be met before the programme can start, such as to revise the documentation, to clarify the mentoring support for students or to modify a module.

Triannual or quinquennial review

At the end of the validation period for a programme (three or five years), it will be reviewed and presented for revalidation. The purpose of the review is to evaluate and make alterations to the programme, so that it is updated and revised to be suitable for the next validation period. This is a time-consuming process, which may take even longer than validation of a new programme because of the evaluative research required by the review.

Step 1: programme review   The programme is extensively evaluated in terms of success in recruitment and retention, student performance and employability, feedback from students, feedback from employers and professional associations, feedback from external examiners on the quality of the programme and the standards of student performance. The review document will also address other factors which will influence the nature of the revised programme, such as institutional strategic plans, changes in institutional infrastructure, markets for potential students, competition from other providers, government agendas and new regulations. All this evaluative information is presented in a review document, which concludes by making recommendations for changes or reforms to the programme.

Step 2: programme development   Informed changes to the programme are made in response to the review such as:

- modifying the aims and learning outcomes;
- modifying the overall programme structure;
- adding, withdrawing or reconfiguring modules;
- altering the mode of delivery;
- changing assessments.

This step may require extensive consultation and planning, if significant reorganisation and development are required; this will take time. The team will write a new validation document, and assemble the usual accompanying documentation necessary for any validation, for example, staff CVs, student handbook, placement or dissertation handbook.

Step 3: validation   The validation event is much the same as that described above, except that the validation panel will need to consider the review document, its recommendations and the case made for continuation of the programme. In validation and review events, the panel will also meet with former and current students, employers of former students, members of professional associations (if appropriate) and senior managers. The purpose of these meetings is to triangulate the information collected on the programme as it has been implemented. The information they gather helps to inform their decision about revalidation and to make constructive conditions or recommendations to the programme team.

Annual monitoring or annual review

As a postgraduate you may not have direct input into programme validation and review. However, you may be involved in annual monitoring if you are teaching, and especially if you have significant responsibilities for a module. As indicated above, annual monitoring is the ongoing quality assurance procedure for assessing the health and wellbeing of the programme and its constituent modules. Annual monitoring reports generally include summary evaluations on:

- learning, teaching and assessment;
- feedback from students, staff, external examiners and others, such as placement supervisors;
- module evaluations;
- statistics on recruitment, retention, pass rates, degree awards, gender and age profiles;
- resources;
- progress on previous year's action plan;
- current year's action plan.

Your input, therefore, will be a part of the module evaluations and feedback from students. This will be particularly significant if you have facilitated all or most of the laboratory or practical sessions, for example.

Find out early if you are expected to contribute to module evaluation. There will probably be a standard evaluation form you should use and you might wish to take time to discuss this with the lecturer or course leader. Most importantly, the feedback you gather will help you reflect on and develop your teaching.

External systems

As we indicated at the beginning of this chapter, the UK agency which regulates and monitors quality in higher education institutions is the Quality Assurance Agency (QAA). You can learn a great deal about the QAA and its remit by visiting its website http://www.qaa.ac.uk. The QAA has set benchmarks for standards of achievement in all major subject areas, so that all stakeholders understand what knowledge and skills can be expected of graduates. It has published codes of practice which set standards in every aspect of educational provision, such as assessment and feedback, recruitment and admissions, and career education.

The QAA also manages systems of periodic external peer review of quality. These systems have evolved over the last decade or so, and are different in various countries of the UK. However, the principles are the same, in that a team of experienced academics, external to the university, assesses and reports on the quality of educational provision. This assessment is usually based on the following activities:

- scrutiny of an institutional report which describes the quality of overall provision and, in particular, quality assurance mechanisms;
- perusal of documents relevant to quality assurance, programme management, assessments, management of marks, records and awards, committee minutes and reports;
- reports from external examiners;
- perusal of students' assessments and feedback at all levels;
- meetings with current and former students;
- meetings with academic and support staff (student services, library, IT);
- meetings with senior managers;
- meetings with employers;
- observation of teaching;
- assessment of learning resources, such as library, IT, laboratories and online resources;
- attendance at committee meetings.

The panel's judgement of quality and standards will be based on a set of criteria set by the QAA and known to the sector. After the panel's visit to the institution, it will publish a report which expresses 'confidence', 'limited confidence' or 'no confidence' in standards and which will also comment on the quality of all other aspects of learning and teaching, with specific reference to examples of good practice and recommendations for consideration by the institution.

Clearly, this is a high-profile activity, and stressful for all staff of the university. The reports are published on the web, and printed copies are circulated to all institutions.

More recently, particularly in Scotland, there has been increasing emphasis on quality enhancement, that is, the actions taken by universities to improve the learning experiences of students which have been deliberate, planned, implemented, evaluated and disseminated. Quality enhancement is a dynamic approach to monitoring quality and is intended to result in continuous improvements, with increased student involvement. The concept of quality enhancement has been welcomed by the sector, and it remains to be seen how effective it will be in stimulating change. It is an approach you might want to keep an eye on as it develops.

Where is your place in all this?

As a facilitator of learning

What is your role in all this? Quality assurance may have little impact on you at the moment, and you may feel you do not need to know any of this just now. However, it is probably a good idea to know the basics so that you have a working knowledge of what it is all about, particularly if you are intending to go into a teaching post at a later stage. In any case, if there is likely to be a review in your department, you may, without any warning, be pulled into a 'chat' with the assessors. It might be as well to have some idea of what is going on and exactly when, in your own department. More importantly, assessors will probably be interested in what preparation you have had for your teaching role. If you have not had any preparation, what answer will you give?

Some of your colleagues may say it is too soon for you to know about quality assurance matters. Some may put it more strongly: do not go there. Certainly, it is good advice to check whether or not you have any active role to play. If you do not and it is still early days in your research programme, maybe this is an area you can leave for later. If you are coming to the end of your research programme and thinking about the next step, it may be time to get involved in a deliberate manner. You can learn more about quality processes in several ways:

- Find out when a programme in your department is up for review and why. Ask what changes are being discussed and why. What are the project plans and deadlines?
- Observe a validation event.
- Join as a 'student' member of the programme team or the validation panel. As part of the quality enhancement initiative, students are positively encouraged to get involved.
- Ask for responsibility to collect and summarise module evaluations.

As a module coordinator or module leader

The day-to-day management of modules is usually handled by a module coordinator or module leader. Generally, this is interpreted to mean the person who has responsibility for administration, teaching, assessment and evaluation. Normally, although postgraduates may teach and/or participate in assessment, they do not have administrative responsibility for the module.

Some (usually more experienced) postgraduates have told us they have been asked to act as module coordinator. If this is true for you, you will be expected to manage enrolments, keep records, organise teaching, book rooms, put books on reserve in the library, organise laboratories, fieldwork or placements (if they are part of the module), distribute information to students, review assessment specifications, implement assessments, mark and give feedback, organise double-marking or sample moderating, send assessments to the external examiner, communicate with the external examiner, collate and sign off marks, attend exam boards, administer and collate evaluations, write the annual module evaluation summary, respond to students' difficulties – and teach and support students!

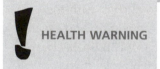 **HEALTH WARNING** Being a module coordinator is a great deal of work. Read the paragraph above again if you are not convinced, and think twice before you agree to take on this responsibility.

This list alone should be enough to warn you that you may have to deal with some serious research-teaching tensions. If you are a part-time postgraduate, perhaps there is more scope for a teaching load of this scale, and indeed, you may be part-funding your degree by teaching. If you are a full-time postgraduate, consider carefully how you will maintain the balance between teaching and research. It may be better to offer to take partial responsibility – for example, doing some of the teaching and some of the marking.

If you do find yourself in the position of having to manage all or part of a module, you may need to know a little of the associated language or terminology. All modules have a number of 'credits' attached to them. Undergraduate modules, for example, may be rated at 10 or 15 credits for a single module. A double module, which would be twice as long, would carry 20 or 30 credits, and a triple module would carry 30 or 40 credits. When an undergraduate successfully completes a module, he or she will be awarded the number of credits associated with that module.

It is worth remembering that the notional number of hours a student can be expected to study is generally 10 times the credit allocation. So a student could expect to put in 100 hours of work for a 10-credit module. Even the honours dissertation and placements are encompassed within the modular system; these activities are normally allocated a high number of credits because of the amount of work involved. Some modules are 'core' for a programme, which means that students are required to take them. Other modules are 'electives' or 'options' and allow students to choose what they would like to study.

Because postgraduates have mentioned a particular dilemma to us, we will deal with it here. What if you don't like the module? What if you disagree philosophically with the organisation, content and/or learning and assessment strategies? Remember, from our discussion above, that your actions are limited. You cannot go in and make major changes just because you don't like what you see. It is quite possible you will be able to change teaching strategies if you think they will enable students to achieve the outcomes more successfully or they will find the learning more motivating. However, alterations to content and assessments must go through formal development and approval processes because they may affect the overall structure of the programme (Moon, 2002).

As a research student

In your role as a research student, you should have an interest in the quality of your own research programme. For interest, and as an introduction to QAA codes of practice, you might like to read the Code of Practice for Postgraduate Research Programmes (QAA, 2004).

The QAA Code of Practice for Postgraduate Research Programmes

- What group developed this code?
- When did it become active?
- What expectations does the QAA have of institutions?
- How many precepts are there?
- What matters do the precepts cover?
- How does your own programme 'stack up' against the precepts?
- How might your institution enhance your research programme?

We have already mentioned one way you might learn more about quality assurance and quality enhancement. Another way, of course, is to cooperate with staff to enhance your own postgraduate programme.

A further alternative is to access other sources of information. The Higher Education Academy (http://www.heacademy.ac.uk), the professional association for teachers in higher education, will give you another window into the multiplicity of issues which surround quality, such as student numbers, competition, retention, professional bodies, student demand, currency of courses, staffing, resources and many others. The Academy also has many links to other useful resources.

Risks of not engaging with quality matters

It is important not to dismiss this as a bureaucratic process. You will hear colleagues, senior and junior, making statements, positive and negative, about QAA and other related processes, both external and internal. Many different groups assess the quality of teaching and learning in universities. Throughout your career, departments will receive written feedback on your teaching from students, and if you have not given time for these systems it will be obvious. Your performance and attitude will be exposed – and that's you 'nailed'.

Portfolio

For you, perhaps the most obvious connection with quality assurance and enhancement is the module. It is most likely you will have been teaching on at least one module, and it will be both important and useful to collect feedback on your teaching as part of the module evaluation. Talk to the programme leader or module coordinator about how you can ask for feedback which will be helpful to you specifically. This may mean that you will have to add a question or two which focuses on your role in teaching and/or assessment.

Also think about how you can collect ongoing feedback on your teaching, which could be collated to inform the overall module evaluation. We have already mentioned several methods for doing this in Chapters 2–6.

If you get more involved in quality processes by observing or participating in them, your notes and reflections on those events would make excellent entries into

your portfolio. Here are some questions to start you thinking what you might
provide evidence on.

- What did you observe about the processes?
- What was your own involvement?
- What was your contribution?
- What did you learn from the processes?
- What did you learn from the final 'event'?

10

Feedback on Your Teaching and Continuing Professional Development

Ideally, a person who is seeking an initial tenure-track faculty position should provide evidence of both research and teaching competence. (Olson and Perkins, 1993: 89)

Three core issues provide a focus for this chapter:

- learning about teaching and learning;
- knowing if what you did in your teaching was good or bad;
- using some kind of model of reflection and professional development to take stock of your progress and plan further development.

You have to have some way of making these into a coherent process, and there are many models out there of 'reflective practice', and its role in continuing professional development (CPD). Many professional groups now specify a framework for CPD, and if your profession does that, then that is the one you should use.

For your first attempt at creating a teaching portfolio, and if there is no clear steer from your department, keep it simple. Figure 10.1 shows that reflection does not just mean sitting down to have a good long think about things; it should have an outcome. Reflection identifies your development needs. If you are not sure what they are, discuss this with a more experienced colleague, or someone in staff development or your head of department, who will have experience of producing and responding to development plans.

The figure also shows the relationship between reflection and CPD: you need to be engaging in both, and it has to be a continuous and circular practice. The purpose of this model is to make explicit the way that reflection lets you identify your development needs, and then development prompts reflection on what you learned, how you moved forward and how far this has taken you towards meeting your needs. This in turn helps you to define your next development goal.

FIGURE 10.1
A model for reflective professional development

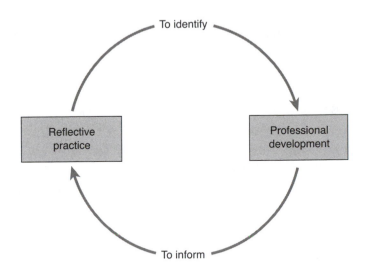

One way of looking at it is that, just as your discipline is always moving forward, teaching is always moving forward, and your teaching knowledge and practice should be moving forward too. You need to be aware of new developments, and you need to move forward in a way that makes sense to others and to yourself.

For your CPD: you can start writing now

- Analyse the model: can you make it relevant to your teaching?
- Is it familiar in your discipline? To your colleagues?
- Do you have notes on discussion of it with more experienced colleagues?
- Are there alternatives?
- Is 'model' the right word for you and for your discipline?

Because reflection is by its very nature a subjective activity, it is helpful to collect information about your practice on which you can reflect. Evidence provides a degree of objectivity about your own practice. You can take a step back. The result is that while your own impressions of your teaching can give you a misty view, because it is by its nature subjective, the evidence you collect or the feedback from someone else can give you a clearer view. This, in turn, can build your confidence in the teaching role. If, alternatively, you have neither evidence nor feedback, your confidence may be eroded: how will you know you did a good job?

Because this is so important, this chapter describes the kinds of evidence that you can collect for yourself. We have selected some that will not be hugely time-consuming and some that are straightforward to collect. Collecting different types of evidence will allow you to triangulate it: evidence from yourself, evidence from your students and evidence from your colleagues, peer and mentors (Day, 1995). We also suggest ways to make your evaluation of your teaching appropriate to the teaching activity.

Collecting evidence yourself

You usually have a 'feel' for how a class has gone, but, of course, that is not enough for you to really gauge whether or not it has gone well. You need some way of at least checking how your 'feel' relates to your students' experience of your teaching.

Get help to develop these approaches from staff development or the teaching and learning centre, from experienced colleagues or designated mentors in your department.

- Teaching diary: you can keep a record of what you do, your rationales and reflections, student responses, what their responses reveal.
- Videotaping a practice session, followed by discussion with peers, sometimes called 'micro-teaching', might make you nervous, but is generally evaluated as the most useful development activity. You can set up the video in your class to give yourself feedback, but remember also to explain and ask permission of students since they may appear on film.
- Audiotaping, particularly if there is something in your voice or speech that you want to work on.
- Informal notes: making notes directly onto your lecture notes to yourself.
- Self-observations: make notes.
- Personal pro forma; could be electronic.
- Keeping a file, getting organised, looking at others' files.

- Checklists to keep you focused.
- Learning log: note learning goals and achievements.

Use the 'portfolio' sections at the end of Chapters 1 to 9, to prompt your writing on the subjects of teaching and learning. There is potentially plenty for you to write about, and the process of simply logging your thoughts and actions could be more valuable than you might think. It lets you create a body of material that you can come back to later.

Collecting evidence from your students

You can do ongoing evaluation, during your course. This gives you a chance to act on student feedback. Even if your department has a formal course evaluation form, distributed at the end of every course or module, you do not have to, and probably should not, wait till the end of the course to get feedback from your students.

In each of the chapters of this book, we have suggested methods for collecting feedback from students. There are also other resources you can use for ideas (Cowan, 1998; George and Cowan, 1999; Day et al., 1998). The following discussion explains, in more depth, the multiple ways that a simple approach can be used to suit your purpose.

Perhaps one of the best and easiest methods for eliciting student feedback, and providing evidence of learning, is the one-minute paper (Angelo and Cross, 1993; Harwood, 1996). This is where you simply ask students one or two questions right at the end of your class. While it might take one minute for them to write it, you might need five minutes to get all their responses in before they leave. You can give them index cards or Post-its for their answers or ask them to write on a piece of paper. You can prompt them to write no more than a sentence. They then hand these in before they leave.

What you do is ask two questions:

1   What was the main point of this class?
2   Do you have any questions?

Alternatively, and/or over time, you can adapt these questions. There are variations that will allow you to find out more about what the students think. For example, for question 1:

- What was the main point of this class?
- What do you think was my main point in this class?

- What, for you, was the main point of the class today?
- How did the main point of today's class relate to the last class?
- What did you learn from this class?

Variations on question 2 can open up areas that students are not sure about, where they may require more information or even revision. Again, there are many ways of asking this question:

- Do you have any questions?
- Have any new questions emerged from this class?
- Do you still have questions about the subject we covered in this class?

You can also repeat this exercise, perhaps in its different forms, over the course of several lectures or labs.

Classroom evaluation: One-minute paper (half-sheet response)

(1–5 minutes before end of the class)

Add your questions here.

This helps students to develop:

- listening skills – students remain attentive;
- ability to think holistically, to integrate ideas;
- reflection on learning/self-evaluation – that is, how well they understood and/or what they recall;
- questioning skills;
- skills of identifying gaps in knowledge;
- understanding of facts, theories, concepts.

While this might seem time-consuming, if you only have large classes, Harwood reports that you can read through as many as 250 responses in less than 30 minutes:

The major benefit of this technique, from my experience, occurs during the first few weeks of the course. At this point, students usually are unsure of the professor and concerned with their ability to handle the course material. Comments are very helpful to me in terms of determining the pace of the course at the outset and in creating the learning atmosphere of the class. (1996: 229)

On the other hand, if you only have small classes, you may think this is a bit artificial: why not just ask the students to say what they think? The answer is that there can be value in anonymity; some students may be more willing to make comments and/or ask questions in this way. Why ask them to write, when they already have so much writing to do? The writing task, short as it is, sometimes lets students articulate something different. They can put some aspect of the class in their own words. Sometimes, new points emerge. Above all, it prompts them to focus on their own thoughts. Even the briefest of responses are helpful: for question 2 you may find that many students write 'no questions' or just leave a blank.

What is interesting here is that you can adapt this technique in order to vary the information you gather and/or to focus on what you want to learn. This has developed into a means of gaining insights into what the students are thinking and how they are adjusting to the new material and the new teacher.

In this example from Harwood (1996), there is no need to evidence the impact of teaching on student learning because the aim is simply to gain insights into the student experience. There is no attempt to do some kind of quantitative analysis of students' responses; that is not what this lecturer is interested in. What is interesting about this approach is that you could use it, particularly at the start of your teaching career, to find out about what students think, what they make of the material. However, you could also use it to find out about any new group you have to teach; so the one-minute paper can be used in a diagnostic way as well.

A variation on this approach is to give the students one minute to compare what they wrote, before they hand their answer(s) in to you. That way, some will see that they are not alone in having questions. They will probably find that some of them have the same questions, and this can be interesting. It might be something you want to discuss at a future class.

As you analyse their responses, if you find, for example, that 50% of the class has raised the same question, that may tell you something about how the students are learning. It might identify areas where they are having difficulties. You might not be able to find this out in any other way, not in terms of the responses of the whole group.

When you then deal with one or two of their questions in your next class, your students will see that you take their questions seriously, that they can address questions to you that matter to them, and even that they can ask you what might be considered 'obvious' or 'stupid' questions in this format, without risking revealing their confusion or misunderstanding. This is an important step for students, since they often report that they never see any response to their feedback on teaching, particularly if their feedback is gathered at the end of a course.

Of course, you do not have to answer every single question, but you might want to put your rationale for your selection in your diary or log. As you use this technique more often, you will learn how to vary the questions and perhaps the format in order to find out more about student learning. You should document this. You might also find that one variation does not work so well. Again, this is important to note and reflect on. It might be time to consult someone else about why it did not work so well. In other words, this form of feedback can be connected to other activities and discussions. It is up to you to make these connections. Let others know that you are using the one-minute paper. Have they used it? What happened? Are the students likely to get a bit bored of it, if everyone starts using it? What can you do to avoid that?

If you do any of the work covered in this section, make sure that you document what you do: be factual. Save your judgements for later. Of course, you will have your own views, but it is important to note observations at this stage. Your purpose should be as much to produce a record of your work as a commentary.

Document your work: show the process you used

- You used this form of evaluation in the recommended manner.
- You read up on the rationale for this approach to student feedback.
- You focused your reading.
- You implemented it carefully.
- You summarised the responses.
- You addressed them in a follow-up discussion.

It might also be important to make your selection explicit to students: it might be important to them to know which questions you decided not to answer and why that was. If, for example, you decided that they could find answers to some of their questions in course materials or websites, then it is clearly important that you say so to them as soon as possible.

As you take stock of your evaluations, think about what you are using evaluation for:

- to find out about learning?
- to improve your teaching?
- to engage the students?
- to diagnose your strengths and weaknesses?
- to investigate student difficulties?
- to provide evidence of your commitment to teaching?
- to provide evidence of your professionalism to interview panels?

You have to be careful not to look for too much at this stage. You also have to think about whether your method of evaluation matches your goal. The example we use in this section – the one-minute paper – is good for achieving what most postgraduates say they want: to get some feedback from students while also stimulating students to engage with course content. Depending on how you use it, it could achieve several of the above goals.

Collecting evidence from peers, colleagues and mentors

You can use peers as sources of evaluative information about your teaching and your students' learning, through observations of teaching and of your students' responses. Many universities have a peer observation scheme designed to give constructive feedback to new lecturers, so ask about how you might benefit from this process. Peers and experienced colleagues also give you feedback by looking at your students' work. Ask peers and experienced colleagues to review your teaching materials. Ask if you can review others' materials. If you are team teaching, and if you are looking for feedback, ask.

Gathering information about teaching

There are journals, websites, books to help you learn more about teaching. Because your time is limited, you will need to choose carefully – to focus (see below). It is probably not a realistic goal, at this stage in your career, to attempt to develop an in-depth knowledge of an area. Instead, you can rely on the types of journals that combine theory and practice to give you an accessible body of knowledge. Be clear about what you can and cannot do, while you are still working on your doctorate.

Choose a focus

- Focus on one form of teaching.
- Select papers on teaching and learning in your discipline.
- Attend a conference on teaching in your discipline.
- Search for websites on teaching in your area

As always, recording is paramount.

Record your reading, assess your learning

- Summarise your reading about methods of collecting evidence.
- Summarise brief discussion(s) with more experienced colleagues on these.
- Select one or two that make most sense or seem most feasible.
- Critique one or two: unrealistic, unscientific, too subjective?
- Sketch how you might implement one.
- Discuss with colleagues; summarise key points.

Your teaching portfolio

After you have collected the evidence, what exactly do you do with it? Simply logging what you do and what you observe is a good start; it should not be seen as too simplistic, but as an important step in the process of becoming a teacher. Moreover, you may not yet have collected enough teaching experiences to know how to judge your performance, and it is when you have collected a set of narratives, observations, plans and notes on your teaching that you can look over it as a body of work.

For example, when you look back, you may be intrigued by your account of how you prepared for your first class. You may be surprised by some of the observations you made during your first few classes. You may find that you have quite quickly changed your views on certain aspects of teaching and learning. Or you may realise that you have developed an emerging set of views on what does and does not work. These views are particularly worth reflecting on subjectively and in discussion with others.

Throughout this book, at the end of each chapter, we suggested many different ways in which you could document your teaching activities in a portfolio. In this section we suggest how you can pull all these elements together, to create a coherent picture of your ongoing development as a teacher.

How postgraduates can use a teaching portfolio

- To describe achievements.
- To inform others of your goals.
- To convince others of the quality of your teaching.

If you have been doing even some of the activities we suggested in the 'portfolio' sections, then you probably already have the components of a teaching portfolio. For example, if you completed one portfolio task per chapter, you will have more than enough. Even if you are not actively involved in all the forms of teaching covered in this book, you can still give an account of your reading and thinking about the subjects. Alternatively, you may have focused on one or two chapters and have invested a bit more time and effort on the portfolio section of those. Your next step is to gather together all your material and make it into a coherent record of your development.

For your teaching role, you have to be able to demonstrate not only that the students were happy with what you did – giving you good scores on evaluation forms, for example – but also that you made sensible decisions about how you did your teaching. Even a novice teacher has access to information and advice about teaching. You have to show how you have accessed that and what decisions you made about how to teach. Even if you had limited choice, in terms of teaching style and content, you still have to have some way of assessing your performance. In addition, you can show that you have a developing understanding of how students learn in your field.

It is your responsibility to look back at what you did and learn something from it. Your teaching portfolio is where you demonstrate what you have learned. In fact, sometimes it is during the process of creating a portfolio that you realise what you have learned. This will serve multiple purposes:

- helping you engage in a continuous process of reflecting on practice and identifying personal development needs;
- providing evidence for quality assurance and enhancement processes, which are departmental and institutional;
- producing a professional portfolio, which can provide evidence for membership of professional bodies;
- continuing accreditation with professional bodies, or subject-specific professional bodies, job applications and promotion.

Increasingly, professional bodies, not just universities, are looking for professional portfolios, some in different aspects of professional work. If you get the hang of this now, you may find it much more straightforward if you have to do something like this at some stage in the future, perhaps in addition to your teaching portfolio.

How will your portfolio be assessed?

- Who is it for?
- Who will read it?
- Do they have stated criteria?
- Do they have specific expectations?
- Do they require specific components?
- Are there sections for teaching achievements and ongoing questions?
- Do you know the kinds of thinking and writing they are looking for?
- For example, is the first element a 'teaching philosophy'?
- Is this only about attitudes and values or also about performance and goals?

Your teaching portfolio – or getting into the habit of developing one – can be used either now or later:

- to identify your strengths and development needs;
- as a personal record of your achievement and development;
- to collect evidence which can support your application for a job, promotion, or tenure;
- as supportive evidence of your application for membership of professional bodies.

In other words, creating a teaching portfolio can help you, in that it makes you take a sensible, diagnostic overview of your teaching and identify your strengths and weaknesses, and it can help others, giving them evidence of your professional approach to teaching. This is also good for your department and your institution. Ultimately, it should also be good for your career. At the very least, it should reduce your doubts about what you are doing.

Portfolio summaries

Table 10.1 summarises the topics we covered in the portfolio sections of the previous chapters. The aim is not to create a comprehensive list of things for you to do now; instead, you should select some of the 'development activities' and document them as 'portfolio materials'. The column on the right includes items that you can put in a teaching portfolio. Some of these you will have already, like lesson plans; others you will have to produce short reports for, such as summaries of discussions and comments on how you can relate them to your teaching.

The layout of the table shows potentially linked activities and materials, but in reality you could link many of the items in the 'activities' column with different items in the 'materials' column. It is up to you.

The purpose of this table is to help you to see the big picture. It is much more than you need at this stage, but it lets you see where this is all going.

As you work through this summary, note that the process of recording your experiences and achievements, with your rationales and evaluations, is only one step in the reflective process. The second, equally important, but sometimes overlooked, step is to generate new questions or to identify recurring questions.

This is because reflection – and other development activities – cannot produce answers to all your questions about teaching and learning; nor does it help you to find solutions to all your teaching problems or issues. Instead, it will almost certainly generate new questions or leave certain causal connections impossible to verify. Reflection should allow you to recognise that you have only partially answered your questions. There are so many variables in any teaching situation – variations in the student cohort, motivation and background, time, your role and performance, other lecturers' influence, use of textbook and technology, and so on – that what worked for one context, for one class, is not guaranteed to work with every other class. Similarly, explaining why something worked, or did not work, when there are so many variables is almost impossible, unless you learn educational research methods. It is, therefore, difficult to evidence that something you did in your teaching 'improved student learning' or 'improved student performance'.

TABLE 10.1
Putting your portfolio together: activities and evidence

DEVELOPMENT ACTIVITIES	PORTFOLIO MATERIALS
Introduction	
Read definition of portfolio	University/other guidelines
Set up file	University/other template
Find criteria for membership/promotion	Notes and comments
Discuss with experienced staff/mentor	Notes and implications
Define teacher development	List and select opportunities
Develop plan with rationale	Copy to file
Answer questions listed	Reflections, plans, questions
Chapter 1	
Read about teaching and learning	Summaries and references
Absorb current thinking	List issues and approaches
Learn about current issues	Learning narratives
Read about learning styles	Description of own style
Discuss teaching and learning	Descriptions of strategies
Learn specialist terms and discourse	Definitions and examples
Relate theory to practice	Discussion: summarise
Focus on area of interest	Report: information gathered
Chapter 2	
Document your lecturing process	Describe steps
Develop lecture plans	Include with comments
Self-assess your performance	Describe what happened
Consider student participation	Describe behaviours
Assess achievement of teaching goal	Describe student responses
Involve students	Student self-assessment
Diagnose areas for change	Describe and justify
Collect feedback: colleagues/students	Summarise and discuss
Review feedback with colleagues	Discuss and summarise

TABLE 10.1   (CONTINUED)

DEVELOPMENT ACTIVITIES	PORTFOLIO MATERIALS
Chapter 3	
Define evidence of impact of teaching	List of definitions
Review teaching–learning relationship	Summaries of reading
Identify evaluation questions	Notes: discuss and evaluate
Assess effectiveness	Definition of criteria
Conduct evaluation	Use of forms, total responses
Demonstrate effectiveness	Institutional format
Identify external benchmarks	Literature/web search
Align with professional body	Summary and discussion
Establish personal goals	List of themes, discussion
Step back: align with outcomes	Description of links
Respond: discuss possible outcomes	Description and selection
Chapter 4	
E-tutoring	Definition and rationale
Assess impact	Description of evaluation tool
Review findings	Analysis and description
New/traditional	Summary of debate
Define/refine skills	Account of implementation
Evaluate	Description and rationale
Assess feasibility	Calculate time required
Align with department goals	List of links
Chapter 5	
Teach lab or fieldwork	Definition and rationale
Identify new challenges	Summary and strategy
Review: stimulating independent thinking	Notes and questions
Document your experience	Lesson plans, observations
Seek feedback	Student /peer evaluation
Discuss feedback	Summary and plan
Keep teaching diary/log	Notes made during teaching
Use questions in this chapter	Answers and explanations
Use/adapt existing template	Record and questions
Chapter 6	
Review forms of evidence	List and illustrate
Observe student behaviours	Description and narrative
Note student performance	Contributions and marks
Start /add to learning log	Your observations/learning
Answer questions listed	Answers and explanations
Identify remaining questions	List and discuss

(Continued)

TABLE 10.1   (CONTINUED)

DEVELOPMENT ACTIVITIES	PORTFOLIO MATERIALS
Chapter 7	
Research support services	List contacts
Learn about legislation	Literature/web searches
Attend staff development	Discuss in your department
Chapter 8	
Take on a new role	Document meetings
Clarify responsibilities	Use of department format
Find out more about it	Information collected
Document learning	Summaries of debates
Implement it	Description and rationale
Reflect on your supervisor's practice	Description and discussion
Assess practice	Review discussion records
Assess impact	Discuss with student(s)
Review personal style	'Diagnostic' writing
Contextualise	Compare other style/teaching
Consolidate	Define good practice
Set new goals	Information to collect
Chapter 9	
Review quality assurance of module	Notes and comments
Discuss with module leader	Record and comments
Review feedback mechanism	Feedback form and notes
Adapt form/add questions	Definition and rationale
Collect feedback	Summary and questions
Observe quality processes	Summary and questions
Answer questions listed	Answers and explanations
Chapter 10	
Review models of CPD	Select and implement
Integrate your teaching	Define department strategy
Overview experiences and materials	Write analysis
Set new goals	Plan reading and activities

This is why some of the 'portfolio materials' column in the table includes, from time to time, prompts for you to generate new questions. It is not just because you are inexperienced in this teaching role that you have new and/or persistent questions; instead, continuous questioning, as for research, is a sign of continuing inquiry. Your record of this type of thinking will be an important form of 'evidence' for your portfolio. If there are no recurring questions or no new questions, your portfolio will seem unrealistic, possibly naive and incomplete.

Over time, however, you may find that simply 'describing' your teaching and 'listing' your observations comes to seem less and less purposeful. While these activities produce a body of material that you can then analyse, you may find that you want to assess your teaching more rigorously. Be careful with this. In order genuinely to assess the impact of your teaching on your students you would have to take account of many variables, you would probably need several different types of data, and it is likely the analysis would have to be longitudinal. What you can do is take a 'diagnostic' view of your teaching:

- Where do you need to make changes?
- How do you know?
- Why?
- What will that mean in practice: what will you actually do differently?
- How will you assess whether or not that made a difference?

While there are many, many things that can go into a teaching portfolio, you should probably have in mind a much shorter list of options (see box). Otherwise, it will take up too much of your time. At a later stage in your career you can add to this list.

What postgraduate teachers can put in a teaching portfolio

The course/class

- Statement of your roles and responsibilities.
- Statement of approaches used in your department.
- List of courses/classes you taught and student numbers.
- Course materials you used: syllabus, handouts, presentations.
- Any new materials you used, with rationale, observations on its use.

Analysis and comment

- Summaries of student behaviour/response/performance.
- Summary of student evaluations of your teaching.

- Comments from peers and mentors.
- Reviews of books, journals or websites on teaching and learning.

Synthesis and diagnosis

- Your synthesis of all this material.
- Statement of your strengths and weaknesses: new goals.

The list is designed to be practical and feasible for postgraduates who teach during their doctorates. You could make extending this list of options, finding out about other possibilities for your teaching portfolio, once you have finished your doctorate, one of your future goals.

CPD: next steps

What counts as CPD in your discipline at this time? What courses are available? What other forms of development are there? How will you evidence improvements in your teaching?

The core activities continue to be:

- Set new development goals.
- State your rationale for them.
- Summarise your evidence that you need to work towards these goals.
- Identify gaps, needs, errors in your teaching practice.
- Put all this in your portfolio.

Keep updating. Check websites regularly, particularly those of established organisations with a focus on the graduate student or postgraduate experience, as they are likely, at this time, to have something on teaching.

- UK Council for Graduate Education: www.ukcge.ac.uk.
- National Postgraduate Committee: www.npc.org.
- Higher Education Academy: www.heacademy.ac.uk.

There will be one main organisation that oversees accreditation of higher education teachers. These and other organisations provide information that may be generic or discipline-specific. Adapt the generic material to your discipline; implement the discipline-specific material and evaluate. Record your observations and any other data.

Once you have some experience of teaching, you can pass on the lessons you learned to others: share teaching resources, discuss difficult situations, share ideas about teaching portfolios. There is some evidence that lack of support is what postgraduates find most 'unhelpful' (Rust, 1991: 35), and that is something that you can rectify: even with limited experience of teaching, you can offer support to others who are just starting.

Once you have helped others in this way, that too can be logged in your portfolio. What exactly did you feel able to contribute? Was there anything that you learned from them? Did they ask questions that you cannot yet answer, and what did you decide to do about that, if anything?

References

Alexander, S. and Boud, D. (2001) 'Learners still learn from experience when online', in J. Stephenson (ed.), *Teaching and Learning Online*. London: Kogan Page.

Allison, I. (1995) 'Demonstrating', in F. Forster, D. Housell and S. Thompson (eds), *Tutoring and Demonstrating*. Sheffield: Centre for Teaching, Learning and Assessment, University of Edinburgh and Universities' and Colleges' Staff Development Agency (UCoSDA).

Angelo, T. and Cross, P. (1993) *Classroom Assessment Techniques*, 2nd edn. New York: Jossey Bass.

Ausubel, D.P. (1968) *Educational Psychology: a Cognitive View*. New York: Holt, Rinehart & Winston.

Bandura, A. (1986) *Social Foundations of Thought and Action*. Englewood Cliffs, NJ: Prentice Hall.

Biggs, J. (2003) *Teaching for Quality Learning at University*, 2nd edn. Buckingham: SRHE and Open University Press.

Biggs, J. and Moore, P. (1993) *The Process of Learning*. Sydney: Prentice Hall.

Black, P. and Wiliam, D. (1998) 'Assessment and classroom learning', *Assessment in Education*, 5 (1): 7–74.

Bligh, D. (2001) *What's the Use of Lectures?* 5th edn. Exeter: Intellect.

Boice, R. (2000) *Advice for New Faculty Members: Nihil Nimus*. Boston, MA: Allyn and Bacon.

Boud, D. (1986) *Implementing Student Self-Assessment*. Sydney: Higher Education Research and Development Society of Australia.

Boud, D. (2000) 'Sustainable assessment: rethinking assessment for the learning society', *Studies in Continuing Education*, 22 (2): 151–67.

Boud, D., Dunn, J. and Hegarty-Hazel, E. (1986) *Teaching in Laboratories*. Milton Keynes: SRHE and Open University Press.

Brockbank, A. and McGill, I. (1998) *Facilitating Reflective Learning in Higher Education*. Buckingham: SRHE and Open University Press.

Brookfield, S. and Preskill, S. (1999) *Discussion as a Way of Teaching: Tools and Techniques for University Teachers*. Buckingham: SRHE and Open University Press.

Brown, G. (1978) *Lecturing and Explaining.* London: Methuen.

Brown, G. and Atkins, M. (1988) *Effective Teaching in Higher Education.* London: Routledge.

Brown, G., Bull, J. and Pendlebury, M. (1997) *Assessing Student Learning in Higher Education.* London: Routledge.

Brown, S., Armstrong, S. and Thompson, G. (1998) *Motivating Students.* London: Kogan Page.

Buckner, K. and Morss, K. (1999) 'The importance of task appropriateness in computer-supported collaborative learning', *ALT-J*, 7 (1): 33–8.

Chanock, K. (2000) 'Comments on essays: do students understand what tutors write?', *Teaching in Higher Education*, 5 (1): 95–105.

Clarke, A. (2004) *e-Learning Skills.* Basingstoke: Palgrave Macmillan.

Cowan, J. (1998) *On Becoming an Innovative University Teacher: Reflection in Action.* Buckingham: SRHE and Open University Press.

Cowley, S. (2003) *How to Survive your First Year in Teaching.* London: Continuum.

Day, K. (1995) 'Supporting and advising students', in F. Forster, D. Housell and S. Thompson (eds), *Tutoring and Demonstrating.* Sheffield: Centre for Teaching, Learning and Assessment, University of Edinburgh and Universities' and Colleges' Staff Development Agency (UCoSDA).

Day, K., Grant, R. and Hounsell, D. (1998) *Reviewing Your Teaching.* Sheffield: Centre for Teaching, Learning and Assessment, University of Edinburgh and Universities' and Colleges' Staff Development Agency (UCoSDA).

Doyle, C. and Robson, K. (2002) *Accessible Curricula: Good Practice for All.* Cardiff: University of Wales Institute.

Entwistle, N.J. and Ramsden, P. (1983) *Understanding Student Learning.* London: Croom Helm.

Falchikov, N. (2001) *Peer Assessment and Peer Tutoring.* Buckingham: Open University Press.

Forster, F. (1995) 'Tutoring in arts and social sciences', in F. Forster, D. Housell and S. Thompson (eds), *Tutoring and Demonstrating.* Sheffield: Centre for Teaching, Learning and Assessment, University of Edinburgh and Universities' and Colleges' Staff Development Agency (UCoSDA).

George, J. and Cowan, J. (1999) *A Handbook of Techniques for Formative Evaluation.* London: Kogan Page.

Gibbs, G. (1990) 'Improving Student Learning Project: briefing paper'. CNAA/Oxford Centre for Staff Development.

Gibbs, G. (1999) 'Using assessment strategically to change the way students learn', in S. Brown and A. Glasner (eds), *Assessment Matters in Higher Education.* Buckingham: Open University Press. pp. 45–54.

Habeshaw, S., Habeshaw, T. and Gibbs, G. (1984) *53 Interesting Things To Do in Your Seminars and Tutorials.* Bristol: Technical and Educational Services.

Harwood, W.S. (1996) 'The one-minute paper', *Journal of Chemical Education*, 73 (3): 229–30.

Heywood, J. (2000) *Assessment in Higher Education: Student Learning, Teaching, Programmes and Institutions.* London: Jessica Kingsley.

Honey, P. and Mumford, A. (1982) *The Manual of Learning Styles.* Maidenhead: Peter Honey.

Jacques, D. (2000) *Learning in Groups*, 3rd edn. London: Kogan Page.

Jarvis, P. (2004) *Adult Education and Lifelong Learning: Theory and Practice*, 3rd edn. London: Routledge Falmer.

Jarvis, P., Holford, J. and Griffin, C. (2003) *The Theory and Practice of Learning.* London: Kogan Page.

Juwah, C., Macfarlane-Dick, D., Matthew, B., Nicol, D., Ross, D. and Smith, B. (2004) *Enhancing Student Learning through Formative Feedback.* The Higher Education Academy.

Knight, P. (1995) *Assessment for Learning in Higher Education.* London: Kogan Page.

Knight, P.T. (2002) *Being a Teacher in Higher Education.* Buckingham: SRHE and Open University.

Kolb, D. (1984) *Experiential Learning.* New York: Prentice Hall.

Laurillard, D. (2002) *Rethinking University Teaching: A Conversational Framework for the Effective Use of Learning Technologies*, 2nd edn. London: Routledge Falmer.

McAlpine, I., Koppi, T., McLean, J. and Pearson, E. (2004) 'Courseware developers as students: a designer perspective of the experience of learning online', *ALT-J*, 12 (2): 147–62.

McConnell, D. (2005) 'Examining the dynamics of networked e-learning groups and communities', *Studies in Higher Education,* 30 (1): 25–42.

McDonald, B. and Boud, D. (2003) 'The impact of self-assessment on achievement: the effects of self-assessment training on performance in external examinations', *Assessment in Education*, 10 (2): 209–20.

Mann, S.J. (2005) 'Alienation in the learning environment: a failure of community?', *Studies in Higher Education*, 30 (1): 43–55.

Marton, F. (1988) 'Describing and improving learning', in R.R. Schmeck (ed.), *Learning Strategies and Learning Styles.* London: Plenum.

Marton, F. and Saljo, R. (1976a) 'On qualitative differences in learning. I: Outcome and process', *British Journal of Educational Psychology*, 46: 4–11.

Marton, F. and Saljo, R. (1976b) 'On qualitative differences in learning. II: Outcome as a function of the learner's conception of the task', *British Journal of Educational Psychology*, 46: 115–27.

Marton, F., Hounsell, D. and Entwistle, N. (1997) *The Experience of Learning: Implications for Teaching and Studying in Higher Education*, 2nd edn. Edinburgh: Scottish Academic Press.

Mason, R. (2001) 'Effective facilitation of online learning: the Open University experience', in J. Stephenson (ed.), *Teaching and Learning Online*. London: Kogan Page.

Mayes, T. and Fowler, C. (1999) 'Learning technology and usability: a framework for understanding courseware', *Interacting with Computers*, 11: 485–97.

Means, B. and Haertel, G.D. (eds) (2004) *Using Technology Evaluation to Enhance Student Learning*. New York: Teachers College Press.

Moon, J. (1999) *Reflection in Learning and Professional Development*. London: Kogan Page.

Moon, J. (2002) *The Module and Programme Development Handbook*. London: Kogan Page.

Moon, J. (2004) *A Handbook of Reflective and Experiential Learning: Theory and Practice*. London: Routledge Falmer.

Nomdo, G.J. (2004) 'Collaborating within the "risk zone": a critical reflection', *Active Learning in Higher Education*, 5 (3): 205–16.

O'Leary, J. (2004) 'Universities are recognizing the growing technological sophistication of students coming to higher education', *Times Higher Education Supplement*, 22 October: 3.

Olson, C. and Perkins, L. (1993) 'Teaching assistant training for general education: a departmental case study', *The Journal of Staff, Program and Organization Development*, 11 (2): 89–96.

Pask, G. (1976) 'Styles and strategies of learning', *British Journal of Educational Psychology*, 46: 12–25.

Prosser, M. and Trigwell, K. (1999) *Understanding Learning and Teaching: the Experience in Higher Education*. Buckingham: SRHE and Open University Press.

Quality Assurance Agency (2004) Code of Practice for the Assurance of Academic Quality and Standards in Higher Education: Postgraduate Research Programmes.

Race, P. (1993) *Never Mind the Teaching, Feel the Learning*. Birmingham: Staff and Educational Development Association.

Ramsden, P. (1988) *Improving Learning: New Perspectives*. London: Kogan Page.

Ramsden, P. (2003) *Learning to Teach in Higher Education*, 2nd edn. London: Routledge Falmer.

Rowntree, D. (1987) *Assessing Students: How Shall We Know Them?*, 2nd edn. London: Harper & Row.

Rust, C. (1991) *Surviving the First Year: the Experiences of New Teaching Staff in Higher Education*. Birmingham: Standing Conference on Educational Development.

Salmon, G. (2002) *E-tivities: the Key to Active Online Learning*. London: Routledge Falmer.

Salmon, G. (2004) *E-moderating: the Key to Teaching and Learning Online*, 2nd edn. London: Routledge Falmer.

(SHEFC) Scottish Higher Education Funding Council (2000) *Teachability: Creating an Accessible Curriculum for Students with Disabilities*. Glasgow: University of Strathclyde.

Seldin, P. (1997) *The Teaching Portfolio: a Practical Guide to Improved Performance and Promotion/Tenure Decisions*, 2nd edn. Bolton, MA: Anker.

Stenglehofen, J. (1993) *Teaching Students in Clinical Settings*. London: Chapman and Hall.

Stephenson, J. (2001) *Teaching and Learning Online*. London: Kogan Page.

Strachan, R., Murray, R. and Grierson, H. (2004) 'A web-based tool for dissertation writing', *British Journal of Educational Technology*, 35 (3): 369–75.

Thow, M. and Murray, R. (2001) 'Facilitating student writing during project supervision', *Physiotherapy*, 87 (3): 134–9.

Tiberius, R.G. (1999) *Small Group Teaching: a Trouble-Shooting Guide*. London: Kogan Page.

Weller, M. (2004) 'Facing a byte-sized future', *Times Higher Education Supplement*, 22 October: 4.

Yorke, M. (2003) 'Formative assessment in higher education: Moves towards theory and the enhancement of pedagogic practice. *Higher Education*, 45 (4): 477–501.

Index

Indexed by Caroline Eley